Discovering BBC Micro Machine Code

How to Get More Speed and Power

A. P. Stephenson

GW00697122

GRANADA
London Toronto Sydney New York

Granada Technical Books
Granada Publishing Ltd
8 Grafton Street, London W1X 3LA

First published in Great Britain by
Granada Publishing 1983
Reprinted 1983, 1984 (3 times)

British Library Cataloguing in Publication Data
Stephenson, A. P.
Discovering BBC Micro machine code.
1. BBC Microcomputer—Programming
I. Title
001.64′04   QA76.8.B3

ISBN 0-246-12160-2

Typeset by V & M Graphics Ltd, Aylesbury, Bucks
Printed and bound in Great Britain by
Mackays of Chatham, Kent

Contents

Preface

Owners of the BBC Microcomputer will be aware of the resident machine code assembler but many will hesitate to use it because they feel it may be far too complicated and unfriendly. It must be admitted that machine code manipulations on most popular micros are far from soothing. This is because the interaction between programmer and machine is usually via a piece of software called a *monitor*. Machine code monitors are very low-level and offer very little help to a programmer. Nothing can be less inspiring than a program listing from a monitor.

The BBC machine is different. Instead of a monitor, it has a full-blooded assembler, which allows you to enter machine code in intelligible form. It is an extraordinary assembler in that it is embedded within the BASIC interpreter, allowing easy transitions back and forth between BASIC and assembler code.

This book may help you to overcome the fear of machine code and to make use of the assembler properties. The exercises are simple, deliberately so, in order to encourage experimentation and to prevent the onset of premature gloom. They are intended to trigger, rather than present, ideas. In keeping with this 'softly-softly' approach, no attempt has been made to present an exhaustive view of the 6502. Some of the more exotic addressing modes like 'indexed indirect' and 'indirect indexed' have been excluded. Such omissions will not be found serious until your abilities in machine code reach the next stage. Some prior knowledge of BASIC, however, as used on the BBC machine has been assumed. Indeed, it would be unwise to plunge straight into machine code without a preliminary 'apprenticeship' in BASIC. The excellent *User Guide* (written by John Coll) which accompanies the machine should be on hand when reading this book.

This book is to be considered the first of two; the second will repair the above omissions, will treat some of the ground again but in more detail and will present more advanced program examples.

A. P. Stephenson

Chapter One
Introducing the Assembler

Why machine code?

Buried inside a ROM in the BBC Microcomputer is one of the most powerful BASIC interpreters likely to be found in machines designed for the home enthusiast. It would take the average beginner, however enthusiastic, several months to realise its full potential because the designers of the ROM have included many advanced structures new to traditional BASIC. The vast BASIC vocabulary is only one of the attractive features. It is also quite a fast interpreter of programs in the *relative* sense.

Nevertheless, however, brilliant the operating system and the language interpreter, there is little point in denying that BASIC is a sluggish high-level language when compared with most other computer languages. The slow execution speed is due to the method of translation. When you write a program in BASIC, it is translated and then executed line by line. However many times you run the same program, the whole laborious business of translation is re-inacted at every line because it is the inherent mechanism of an *interpreter*. The more professional high-level languages use a *compiler* to translate. The essence of a compiled language is the separation of the translation phase from the execution phase. The program is first 'compiled' (translated) into a form the machine understands. This is a once-only operation (see Figure 1.1). The program is then run from this compiled version and, consequently, is a much faster operation. Unfortunately, a language which is compiled, rather than interpreted like BASIC, lacks flexibility and friendliness because it is a difficult task to edit out corrections once it has passed the original translation phase. BASIC was deliberately designed as an *interpretive* language because it was considered that user-friendliness was a more important factor than execution speed. In the last few years, several software firms have designed BASIC

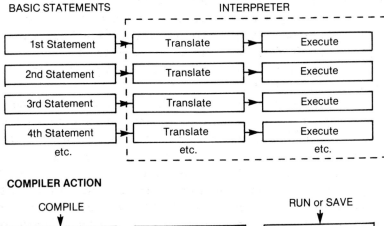

INTERPRETER ACTION

BASIC STATEMENTS   INTERPRETER

1st Statement	Translate	Execute
2nd Statement	Translate	Execute
3rd Statement	Translate	Execute
4th Statement	Translate	Execute
etc.	etc.	etc.

COMPILER ACTION

COMPILE   RUN or SAVE

| SOURCE PROGRAM (Written in high level language) | COMPILER (Translates entire program into machine code) | OBJECT PROGRAM (Complete machine code version) |

Fig. 1.1. Interpreter and compiler action.

compilers and no doubt one of these will be available (if not already) for the BBC machine. Although these will execute much faster, they will still not be able to compete with the speed of *machine code*.

It is never an easy task to seduce confirmed BASIC lovers away from their cosy environment. This is understandable because so much apparent power is available by typing in a few keywords. After all, most programs written in BASIC appear to execute 'instantaneously'. If we try the usual persuasive technique, extolling the speed advantages of machine code, the response may be little more than lukewarm. If a program runs in a few *milliseconds* (and most of them do) there is little to be gained by pointing out that a machine code version would run in *microseconds*. As far as humans waiting for the 'answers' to appear on the screen are concerned, milliseconds are just as instantaneous as microseconds! However, there are some programs which run so slowly in BASIC that machine code versions are practically a necessity. There are two obvious areas which cry out for machine code – *animation* and *input/output control*. There are many popular games portraying moving graphics which would be greatly improved if at least parts of the program were written in machine code. In the field of robotics, it would be virtually impossible to attempt any degree of sophistication by sticking entirely to BASIC. It is easy to make the robot's arm move but for it to *sense* by itself *when* to move it is quite another matter, demanding fairly high processing speed. Those amazing animated diagrams we see on TV science programs in which a complex drawing of, say, an aircraft revolves so as to view it from all angles would be quite out of the question in BASIC. In all fairness, I hasten to add that you will need more advanced textbooks if you are attempting programs of this order of complexity.

So apart from execution speed, which should not be considered the overriding factor in most programs, what other inducements are there for delving into the jungle of machine code? Perhaps this may seem a tame, perhaps pompous statement, but I think the greatest attraction of machine code is the satisfaction derived from using it. Studying machine code, even at an elementary level, helps you to understand how computers work. It gives you the feeling you are really *controlling* the computer instead of just using it. When you write in machine code you know what is going on in the computer at every line. You can almost visualise the bits racing along the printed circuit board. I get much satisfaction from such a simple act as filling the accumulator with a string of 'ones' because it is done *directly* rather than via a faceless chunk of interpretive software. In machine code, you are 'talking' face to face with the *microprocessor*, one of the most advanced pieces of silicon magic ever devised. The BBC Micro uses the 6502 microprocessor in the basic system but allows growth in the form of an add-on unit which contains a second processor. This can be another 6502 or the equally powerful Z80. Indeed, if money is no object, the second processor can be one of the new marvels – the 16/32 bit 16032 which upgrades the BBC machine almost to the status of a minicomputer! This book however is devoted only to the 6502 species although much of the treatment, particularly the details of binary codes and arithmetic processes, is common to other microprocessors.

There is another strong inducement for learning machine code. It tends to be less wasteful of memory although the advantage is unlikely to be felt on small programs.

Assembly code

Up to now, the term 'machine code' has been used loosely so we had better understand the possible meanings attached to what is, after all, a term with two or three meanings. We must distinguish between *binary* machine code, *hexadecimal* machine code and *assembly* code.

(a) Binary machine code

Each instruction to the computer would be a meaningless string of 'ones' and 'zeros'.

Example: 1010 1001 0000 0011 would be an instruction to place the decimal number 3 into the 'accumulator'. Fortunately, this type of machine code is a relic of a bygone age when each tiny bit of information had to be entered from a long row of switches. However, if we could somehow get this pattern into our 6502 microprocessor it would be a valid instruction to perform the above action.

(b) Hexadecimal machine code

Example: A9 03 is the same instruction as defined in the previous example but written in a slightly less formidable fashion. It is called hexadecimal code and, if it weren't for the excellent *assembler* built into the BBC machine, would be our only way to program in machine code.

(c) Assembly code

Example: LDA #3 is again the same instruction. It is an abbreviation for LoaD Accumulator with the number 3. You may agree that this form, although still lacking the friendliness of BASIC, has at least some pretence towards an intelligible code. Thus, A9 in hexadecimal code, which is quite meaningless to humans (except perhaps the code and cypher boffins in MI5), has been replaced by LDA which at least has some mnemonic value.

In this book, our examples will be in assembly code but, when considered helpful, will be supported by hex code. We should first explain that an 'assembler' is not a physical piece of hardware. It is simply a subsection of the operating system resident in one of the ROM chips. It is a program which *helps you to program* in machine code. Amongst other things, it enables you to use three-letter mnemonics (like LDA above) instead of looking up those dreary hex codes (like A9 above). Another advantage is the use of *symbolic* names for addresses instead of hex code addresses. It is also possible to use independently chosen *labels* for destination addresses in 'jump' type instructions. An assembler also provides some assistance in debugging and editing but, unfortunately, the help given is not of the same standard as we are used to in BASIC.

In spite of some shortcomings, owners of the BBC Micro (and its generic ancestor, the Acorn Atom) are lucky to have a resident assembler. Few other microcomputers arrive with assembler facilities. They are normally available from software firms but must be purchased on tape or disk which means that a preliminary load action is required before programming in assembly code. On the other hand, most machines incorporate a 'machine code monitor' but, compared with an assembler, it is a crude substitute. In fact, the absence of an assembler is probably the major reason why few home computer enthusiasts tackle machine code. If only a monitor is available, it is an irksome and painstaking task to program because all those hex codes for each instruction must be memorised or continually looked up. And, because there is no mnemonic content in hex code, it is almost inevitable that many mistakes will be made which are difficult to find. On the other hand, a good assembler – although the program is still fundamentally machine code – minimises the probability of error and makes program writing tolerably pleasant.

How to use machine code

One of the unusual and comforting things about the BBC assembler is the ability to jump easily back and forth from machine code to BASIC. Because it is so easy, beginners in machine code can tackle the subject gently, a few lines at a time, knowing they have the solace of BASIC to return to at any time should the going get tough. In fact, it is probably better for the beginner to tackle machine code in such a piecemeal fashion. In other words, use chunks of machine code sandwiched in between a BASIC program rather than attempt to write the lot in machine code. The great thing is to avoid ambitious programs until you gain confidence.

At the risk of dissuading readers before they have had a chance to progress further, it must be said that machine code demands much study, extraordinary patience and determination! It is an additional benefit if you have (or can acquire) a thick skin to survive the jeers of colleagues when you proudly display your first machine code brain-child. 'Is that all?' is the typical reaction. For the first month, unless you are one of these fortunate individuals who find machine code easy, don't expect to write 'worth-while' programs. Be content to plod on, moving data around between the various registers and memory slots and performing simple arithmetic. It would be unwise to contemplate writing, say, a complex games program with fast-moving graphics as a first exercise.

Where to store programs

When entering a BASIC program, few people show the slightest interest in *where* their program is stored in memory. Indeed, why should they? The resident operating system takes care of all the mundane tasks associated with the storing of variables and program lines. In any case, it would be unwise to leave such decisions, which are fraught with hidden dangers, to the users of BASIC. We should remember that BASIC, in common with many other high-level languages, was designed to cater for the majority of people who just want to *use* a computer without having to bother with the sordid details of computer science.

Students of machine code, however, must be prepared to take considerably more interest in the hidden technical mysteries, particularly in the area of memory 'addresses'. For example, it is practically essential to have a working knowledge of *hexadecimal* code, not simply because it sounds academic but because it is the most concise and logical method of labelling memory locations. In general, the writer of a machine code program is free to store a program starting at any address in the memory map. But freedom carried to excess is anarchy which, in the area of microcomputers, can be catastrophic. The easiest thing in the world to cause the dreaded 'crash' is to locate your program at some arbitrary address. The operating system will then, almost certainly, exhibit symptoms of paranoia and destroy your program.

There are several ways of telling the system where your program is to be stored but, for the moment, we shall consider a simple and reasonably safe method which will not cause a crash by over-writing data in the operating system. There is an area of memory specially reserved for 'user-subroutines' in the BBC computer memory map located at the hex address 0D00–0DFF. There is room for 255 bytes, which doesn't seem much but is adequate for most experimental purposes. (Remember that machine code programs are far superior to BASIC programs with regard to memory efficiency.) It is as well to emphasise this safe area:

The safe area for machine code is 0D00 to 0DFF using hex notation. In decimal terms, this becomes 3328 to 3583.

Perhaps some are wondering at this stage what exactly is 'hex' and may even be a little unsure what a 'byte' is. These terms are usually treated *ad nauseam* in the first chapter of books on machine code, together with scores of other jargon terms. The trouble is that too much of this 'scientific' stuff can be a little off-putting if introduced too early. The terms hex and byte are well defined in the BBC Micro *User Guide* and treated at reasonable depth in my second book, *Get More From BBC Micro Machine Code* (Granada). In any case, you can stick to decimal if you want to because the machine caters for lovers of both number systems. Type on your machine, PRINT &0D00. The machine knows it is hex by the '&' symbol and will immediately print out the decimal equivalent 3328 (which checks with the figures above).

The next important question is, of course, how do you tell the system to store a machine code program starting at the hex address 0D00? This is where the protected variable P% comes into its own. This variable is associated with the most important register in the microprocessor, the *program counter* which is responsible for the smooth sequential execution of your orders. Any number you initialise into P% is interpreted as a *starting point* for the machine code. For example, if we set somewhere at the beginning of the program the line P% = &0D00, the following machine code program will be lodged in a memory block starting at &0D00.

It should be stressed that there are other ways of initialising the program but, until some confidence is gained, stick to our friend 0D00.

Simple machine code program

It may seem premature to discuss a complete program before even describing the actual machine codes but it is hoped that you will key this simple machine code program (Example 1.1) into your computer, if only for practice in interpreting the assembler output.

What does it do? Not very much I am afraid. It just displays the characters ABC round the middle of the screen. Nevertheless, it is a start and well worth studying carefully. It can be divided into three parts, the BASIC program with the machine code routine inside it, the machine code *assembled* and finally the single direct command CALL. Let's analyse the parts separately:

(a) *The BASIC program*
Note that it has the familiar *line numbers* on the left, lines 10 to 130. Line 20 simply ensures MODE 7 and clears the screen. Line 30 is to

```
10 REM *EXAMPLE 1.1*
20 MODE 7:CLS
30 P%=&D00
40 [
50 LDA #65
60 LDX #66
70 LDY #67
80 STA 32320
90 STX 32321
100 STY 32322
110 RTS
120 ]
130 END

>RUN
0D00
0D00 A9 41     LDA #65
0D02 A2 42     LDX #66
0D04 A0 43     LDY #67
0D06 8D 40 7E  STA 32320
0D09 8E 41 7E  STX 32321
0D0C 8C 42 7E  STY 32322
0D0F 60        RTS
```

Example 1.1. Display characters using registers A, X and Y.

inform the system that a machine code program is to be located at
the hex address 0D00. (Note carefully the '&' prefix and also that the
leading '0' in the full address 0D00 can be dropped – it is optional).
Line 40 is short and sweet – the *square* bracket informs the system
that what follows is machine code and the part requiring
'assembling'. Lines 50, 60 and 70 place ('LoaD') data into the
Accumulator, the *X-register* and the *Y-register*. The hash-mark #
defines the numbers as *data* rather than addresses. The numbers
65, 66 and 67 are the ASCII codes for the characters A, B and C
respectively.

Lines 80, 90 and 100 STore the contents of the three registers into
three consecutive addresses. These addresses are permanently
allocated to the Mode 7 screen (around the middle of it). Any
number placed in this area is interpreted as an ASCII code for that
character and the hardware circuitry lights up the screen in the right
place. Only Mode 7 recognises ASCII.

Line 110 is RTS meaning ReTurn from Subroutine. Line 120 is
the square bracket again but in the *closing* position to signal the
completion of the machine code. (Remember that in Mode 7, the

square brackets come out as arrows.) Incidentally, the Mode 7 screen addresses in Example 1.1 are for the model B version. For model A, the addresses are 15376,7,8.

(b) *The assembled version of the machine code*
After the BASIC code is entered and we type RUN, something rather unexpected happens, as you can see from the weird-looking output in Example 1.1. All the command RUN does is to *assemble* the code. It does *not* execute it. The assembly process consists of converting all the mnemonic letter groups into hexadecimal machine code versions called OPERATION CODES and converting any decimal numbers we may have used for *our* convenience into hex to suit the *machine's* convenience. Having completed these conversions, the assembler then stores the resultant code into the RAM area defined by P% and finally displays on the screen a formalised report of its labours. It is this display, shown in Example 1.1, which is the assembled output.

(c) *The command CALL*
As previously stated, the command RUN merely assembles the program. To actually execute it, you must give the command CALL &D00. The result is the appearance on the screen of the characters ABC. (See Figure 1.2 which illustrates assembler action.)

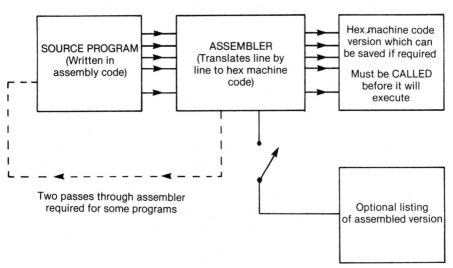

Fig. 1.2. Assembler action.

Making sense of the assembly listing

A casual glance back at Example 1.1 again will confirm that a

certain amount of explanation is called for before it starts to make sense. We will pick one line at random to start with:

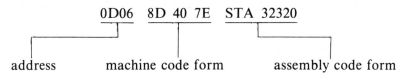

There are, in fact, three separate pieces of information in each line:

(a) *The address*
This is always a four-digit hex number. It is the address in memory where the *first pair* of hex digits in the machine code are located. Thus, in the example line, 8D is in address 0D06. The next pair will automatically be in the next consecutive address. Thus, 40 will be in 0D07 and 7E will be in 0D08. Perhaps it may be understood now why the address column appears to progress in such a disorganised sequence. The address in the row beneath our example is 0D09 which is the next vacant location for the first hex pair (8E) on the next line. The assembly listing is done in this manner because if it were displayed in the way the actual addresses are allocated it would have a toilet roll appearance:

    0D06   8D
    0D07   40
    0D08   7E
    0D09   8E
    etc.

(b) *The machine code*
The first pair of hex digits is the *operation code* (known as the op-code). It is the code, chosen by the designers of the 6502 microprocessor for the action 'load some data into the accumulator' and is 8D. Every instruction has its own unique op-code – there are over seventy of them in the complete repertoire.

The next part of the instruction is called the *operand* which in this case (but not always) happens to be an address in the form of two pairs of hex digits, 40 7E. There are two hex digits in a byte so this particular instruction has a *two byte* address as its operand. (As a point of interest, not all instructions have a two byte operand; some have one and some have no operand at all.)

It is important to note that: *In all two-byte operands, the hex pairs are back to front.* Thus the operand 40 7E should be read as 7E 40. This is confusing for mere humans but where the internal logic of the

6502 microprocessor is concerned, humans are of little importance. If it's better for the machine for the operand to be back to front, then that is all that matters. As a matter of interest, hex 7E 40 is 32320 in decimal.

(c) *The assembly code*

STA 32320 is the way we entered our order to STore the Accumulator in the original BASIC program. (See Figure 1.3 which shows how the program rests in the memory.)

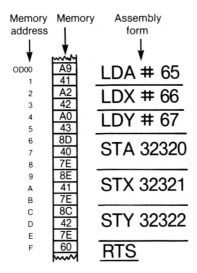

Memory address	Memory	Assembly form
OD00	A9	LDA # 65
1	41	
2	A2	LDX # 66
3	42	
4	A0	LDY # 67
5	43	
6	8D	STA 32320
7	40	
8	7E	
9	8E	STX 32321
A	41	
B	7E	
C	8C	STY 32322
D	42	
E	7E	
F	60	RTS

Fig. 1.3. How the program appears in memory.

The above analysis of the assembler action highlights its advantages. Remember that even though you use the assembler to enter your machine code it is still machine code you are using. All the assembler does is to take a little of the tedium out of the task. Just consider the horrors of writing a program directly in machine code without the help of an assembler.

The op-code and the operand

It is very important to grasp the difference between the op-code and the operand. Since they are component parts of a machine code instruction it is wise to begin with the definition of an *instruction*:

An *instruction* is one complete order to the microprocessor.

Because the microprocessor has an extremely limited 'intelligence', any instruction given to it must be simple, in a strict format with symbols recognised by the assembler. Unlike a *statement* in BASIC, each instruction is 'atomic' rather than 'molecular' in action and consequently doesn't do very much.

Most orders given in real life consist of two parts, the *verb* which informs what particular *action* you want and a *noun* which informs which particular *object* is to receive the action. For example 'kick' is an example of an incomplete order because it is only the verb – there is no indication of who or what is to be kicked. However the order, 'Kick the cat!' is now complete and unequivocal (the fact that it is unkind is irrelevant). Returning now to the question of op-code and operand, we may relate them to the previous sentence. 'Kick' is the op-code and 'the cat' is the operand. However, in similar words to dear old Mrs Beeton's, it may be a case of 'first get your cat'. The cat may not be immediately available – but you may remember *where* it can be found. All this may appear to be useless for understanding assembly code but you will find the analogies may help.

Now examine a real instruction in assembly code:

LDA #20

LDA is the op-code which is a mnemonic for 'LoaD the Accumulator' and is the *verb*. The operand is the number 20, which is 'immediately' available because the '#' sign is the coded information to this effect. Thus the effect is to load (place) the number 20 into the accumulator. If the '#' sign is absent, the operand has a different significance. Instead of being immediately available, the operand is the address in memory *where* the number or data is residing.

Storing a machine code program

Example 1.1, although it contains a section of machine code, is a BASIC program from the operating system's viewpoint. This means we can store it on tape with the usual SAVE"name" procedure and retrieve it later by LOAD"name". But suppose we want only the machine code part? After all, the BASIC part was only to enter the program by means of the assembler so, after this has been done and RUN, the machine code is assembled into the chosen RAM addresses.

To store only the machine code portion, use:

*SAVE"name" SSSS EEEE

where "name" is arbitrarily chosen; SSSS is the *starting address* in hex; and EEEE is the end address plus one in hex.

Suppose we name our machine code part of Example 1.1 BLOGS. The store command would be:

   *SAVE"BLOGS" 0D00 0D10

The start address is easy but the end address may be puzzling. However, if you remember that the last byte in the assembly was in 0D0F and you know enough hex to add 1, this becomes 0D10.

There is an alternative format for storing which saves you the bother of finding out the end address:

   *SAVE"name" SSSS + NNNN

Where NNNN is the number of bytes in the machine code program plus 1. If you count the number of hex pairs in the listing of Example 1.1 you will see there are fifteen, so we want the hex for sixteen which is 0010. Thus, we could save by the command:

   *SAVE "BLOGS" 0D00 + 0010

The exact number of bytes required need not be exact. Providing you order *enough* it doesn't matter if you carry a few garbage bytes along. Guessing, well on the generous side, is slovenly but involves no risk apart from wasting time. In fact, while we continue to use 0D00 as the starting point, there is no reason why the save line couldn't be standardised to:

   *SAVE"name" 0D00 0DFF

This would store the entire reserved memory area and, on my tape machine, only takes about 15 seconds.

Loading a machine code program

To retrieve the program again, the format is: *LOAD"name" or, if you have forgotten the name under which it was stored, simply *LOAD"" (remember there must not be a space within the two quotes). The machine code will then be located in the same memory block as ordered during the original store operation. However, if for some reason (probably not very often) you wish to load it into a different starting address, then use: *LOAD"name" SSSS where SSSS is the starting address required.

Running a machine code program/subroutine

You cannot execute a machine code program (which has just been loaded from tape or disk) by typing the usual RUN. Only a BASIC program understands RUN. However, assuming it is a machine code *subroutine*, it can be executed by CALL &SSSS, where SSSS is the starting address. Our Example 1.1 was of course a subroutine because it ended in RTS, so CALL &0D00 will execute it. However, if the machine code had ended with BRK instead of RTS some rather weird things happen.

BRK means 'break' – stop or break out of the program. It stops dead instead of returning from wherever it was called. Alter line 110 in Example 1.1 from RTS to BRK. When you later try to call it with CALL &0D00 the result is a stream of garbage on the screen. However, if instead of loading the machine code from tape with *LOAD"name" we use *RUN"name" then all is well. The program will load from tape and then automatically execute, producing the expected 'ABC' on the screen followed by the usual winking cursor of BASIC. In spite of this information regarding BRK endings, it should be emphasised that the vast majority of machine code exercises will terminate with RTS. They can then be called from BASIC at any time.

Once a machine code subroutine is *in situ*, it is satisfying to learn it remains unperturbed by hitting the BREAK key. We know that hitting BREAK will destroy BASIC programs (unless it is followed by hitting OLD) but has no effect on any machine code located in a protected area such as 0D00. This is why it is feasible, indeed desirable, to build up a library of machine code subroutines which, providing you know where they are stored, can be called up at any time by either BASIC or by other machine codes.

Symbolic operands

The BBC assembler has quite sophisticated features, including the ability to recognise *symbolic operands*. This is a new piece of jargon but simply means that the operand of a machine code instruction (the hex pair or pairs which follow the op-code) can be a meaningful *name* of your own choice rather than a dry, uninformative hex number. For example, the operand in line 80 of Example 1.1 is 32320 which is an address around the centre of the Mode 7 screen display.

Suppose we chose the name 'Screen' for this number. The complete instruction would then be written as:

8ø STA Screen

However, it may be clear that somehow we must previously inform the assembler that the name 'Screen' must henceforth be associated with the address 32320. In other words, we must assign this in the BASIC part of the program. Once assigned, it is allowable to introduce arithmetic processes to the symbolic operand. Thus, we can rewrite Example 1.1 into an alternative form as shown in Example 1.2.

```
10 REM *EXAMPLE 1.2*
20 MODE 7:CLS
30 P%=&D00
35 Screen=32320
40 [
50 LDA #65
60 LDX #66
70 LDY #67
80 STA Screen
90 STX Screen+1
100 STY Screen+2
110 RTS
120 ]
130 END

>RUN
0D00
0D00 A9 41      LDA #65
0D02 A2 42      LDX #66
0D04 A0 43      LDY #67
0D06 8D 40 7E   STA Screen
0D09 8E 41 7E   STX Screen+1
0D0C 8C 42 7E   STY Screen+2
0D0F 60         RTS
```

Example 1.2. Using symbolic addresses.

Note that the assignment instruction has squeezed in at line 35. There is no doubt that the use of symbolic operands increases the readability and 'friendliness' of machine code and anything that does that should be exploited shamelessly, even if it does waste a few lines for assigning.

Remarks

In BASIC, the keyword REM can be used for explanatory remarks. This is illegal in machine code. However, the BBC assembler allows remarks if preceded by the backward slash (\). This is the key to the left of the 'back-cursor' on the BBC machine. (When in Mode 7, this comes out as a rather funny looking '½'). Example 1.3 shows typical remarks or comments at lines 50, 60 and 70. An alternative to the backward slash is the semicolon.

I have mixed feelings about the over-liberal use of machine code remarks. There are times when a remark on every line makes the program look fiercer than it really is, probably because it is not immediately obvious (as in BASIC) that they are indeed remarks and not valid instructions. Use remarks by all means but only when the intention may not be obvious to those who know a little machine code.

```
 10 REM *EXAMPLE 1.3*
 20 MODE 7:CLS
 30 P%=&D00:REM SET PROG COUNTER
 35 Screen=32320
 40 [
 50 LDA #65 \ ASCII for'A'
 60 LDX #66 \ ASCII for'B'
 70 LDY #67 \ ASCII for'C'
 80 STA Screen
 90 STX Screen+1
100 STY Screen+2
110 RTS
120 ]
130 END

>RUN
0D00
0D00 A9 41    LDA #65 \ ASCII for'A'
0D02 A2 42    LDX #66 \ ASCII for'B'
0D04 A0 43    LDY #67 \ ASCII for'C'
0D06 8D 40 7E STA Screen
0D09 8E 41 7E STX Screen+1
0D0C 8C 42 7E STY Screen+2
0D0F 60       RTS
```

Example 1.3. Using remarks with the backslash.

Multistatements per line

As in BASIC, the colon can be used to separate two or more machine code instructions on the same line. This is a facility which is a mixed blessing and you are strongly advised to ignore it until you can read machine code like reading a book. Unless there is an absolute need to save every byte of memory or save a few inches of printing paper then stick to one instruction per line. It is easier to follow, and any dodge which makes machine code easier is an overriding consideration.

The OPT statement in assembly listing

After typing in one of the previous example programs, a listing is produced on the screen when you type RUN. However, this assembly listing may not always be required. The main purpose of RUN was to *assemble* the mnemonics or symbolic operands into hex machine code; the listing of the result on the screen may be a nuisance. The OPT statement allows individual choice from a range of four options:

OPT 0 Stops the listing and any assembly error reports.
OPT 2 Stops the listing but reports any assembly errors.
OPT 1 Gives a listing but no assembly error reports.
OPT 3 Gives a listing and reports assembly errors.

The statement is not BASIC. It is only valid in the machine code square brackets region.

To see the effect, add the following line in any of the previous examples:

45 OPT 0

When the program is RUN, no familiar assembly listings will appear.

If no OPT statement is given, it assumes OPT 3 which obviously is the form most frequently required during program development.

It will be seen later that some machine code subroutines require assembling twice. In such programs, the poor assembler fails to make head or tail of the listing during the first 'pass' but masters the situation on the second. It would be better to delay discussion on this quirk until later.

Upper-case and lower-case characters

When writing a BASIC program, the BBC allows the use of upper- or lower-case characters for variable names but insists that upper-case is used for BASIC keywords. This is an excellent facility and apart from the added freedom and readability of the listings, it ensures that keywords stand out from variables.

However, when it comes to the machine code part (within the square brackets) the assembler recognises upper- and lower-case not only for operand names but also for machine code mnemonic op-codes! Even mixtures are allowable. Thus, line 60 in the examples could be written as LDX,ldx,lDx or LDx in the op-code position. Personally, I hate this freedom. Machine op-codes have always been written in upper-case, and the manufacturers of microprocessors (including the 6502) have consistently defined the instruction repertoire in upper-case letter groups. I shall never take 'advantage' of the freedom to use lower-case for op-codes and I hope you won't. The effect is awful and confusing!

Practising use of the assembler

This chapter has concentrated on one very simple machine code program with a few variations thrown in. The program, of course, has no practical value and is absurdly simple. Even worse, it is inefficient. But the intention was merely to enable you to get used to the assembler. Try and practice its use for an hour or so for a week. It is hopeless tackling the details of advanced programs unless you can operate the assembler *instinctively*. Try a few simple variations on it. Find out for yourself if you can amend a line direct from the assembly listing using the usual cursor facility. You may find it won't work when you try to execute it. You may find it is necessary to re-list it in BASIC first, before a line can be amended. After a time, you will discover that the BBC assembler is indeed a fine piece of work and marvel that all this power is free – buried in the ROM language interpreter.

Summary

- Machine code executes rapidly, is economical on memory and assists understanding of the inner workings of a computer.

- 'Machine code' is a loose term which covers *binary* machine code, *hexadecimal* machine code and *assembly* code.
- Writing in assembly code is possible only if specialised software is available called an *assembler*. The BBC machine has an assembler in ROM form.
- An assembler allows the use of mnemonic letter groups for the *operation codes*, decimal instead of hex numbers – with symbolic operands and labels.
- Machine code can only be stored in 'safe' areas of memory. One safe area is from 0D00 to 0DFF hex. In decimal, this is 3328 to 3583.
- The BBC assembler operates within a BASIC program but RUN does not execute the machine code; it only *assembles* it.
- An assembly listing is in three parts – the address, the hex machine code and the equivalent assembly 'language' form.
- An instruction consists of the *op-code* and, in most cases, an *operand*.
- A machine code segment, lying within a BASIC program, can be stored on tape or disk separately.
- A machine code segment is not destroyed by operating the BREAK key once.
- Providing a machine code segment is a *subroutine* (it ends with RTS) it can be executed by CALLing it; i.e. CALL &0D00.
- Symbolic operands can only be used if previously assigned.
- Arithmetical expressions can be used in operands.
- Remarks are allowed on assembly lines providing they are prefixed by a backward slash (\).
- As in BASIC, the *colon* can be used to separate two or more instructions on the same line.
- Assembly listings can be modified or omitted altogether by use of OPT.
- Upper- or lower-case characters can be used for op-codes.

Chapter Two
Number Representation

There are two entirely different types of computer, depending on the method used to represent and manipulate numbers. The *analogue* computer represents a number by relating it to the magnitude or intensity of a physical quantity (see Figure 2.1). The physical quantity chosen is usually, but not necessarily, electrical voltage. Number representation could be achieved by using a voltage scaling factor of, say, one millivolt per unit. Then the number 45 would be simulated by a voltage of 45 millivolts. The actual scaling factor is unimportant providing there is consistency in the system. The BBC machine, like all other home computers, is a digital computer but, because an *analogue to digital converter* (AD converter) is provided on the circuit board, it is important not to despise analogue techniques. Digital computers have all the glamour in the modern world, mainly because the popular press considers the analogue type of little news value. Nevertheless, many so-called high technology systems include substantial areas of analogue computing techniques intermixed with digital. Unfortunately for the poor old analogue computer it has one major drawback which makes it quite unsuitable for commercial calculations. It has a low standard of accuracy. It is fast, indeed much faster than the most powerful mainframe digital computer but it has great difficulty in displaying results to greater than four decimal figures with *consistency*. Thus it couldn't have handled the late Howard Hughes' bank account.

Why is the digital computer so accurate and the analogue not so? The answer lies in the difference between *counting* and *measurement*. The digital computer is essentially a counting machine. It is always possible to count accurately. It is impossible, even in the most sophisticated machine, to measure accurately because it will always be dependent on the 'accuracy' of the measuring standard. You cannot measure, say, 5 volts with absolute accuracy but you can say with absolute certainty whether a voltage *is* there or *not* there. You

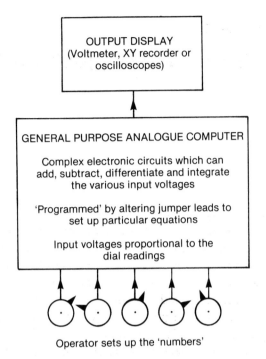

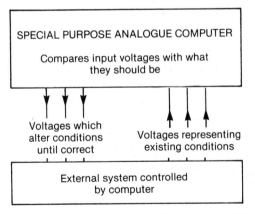

Fig. 2.1. General and special purpose analogue computers.

can tell whether a switch is ON or OFF. Digital computers rely on detecting whether a 'switch' is ON or OFF. In fact, a digital computer is nothing more than a gigantic bank of switches – not the type of switch you can handle physically, of course, but tiny electrical circuits which are *two-state*, either in one state or the other. By counting the number of circuits in the ON state, it is possible for the computer to treat the result numerically.

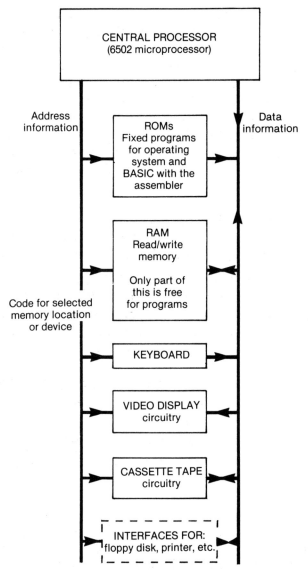

Fig. 2.2. Simplified block diagram of the BBC Micro (a *digital* computer).

Figure 2.2 shows a simplified block diagram of the BBC Micro as an example of a digital computer.

Binary

Binary is a two-state counting system using only two characters 1 and 0 and is therefore the system of choice. It may be tedious for humans, used to ten characters 0,1,2,...9 but tedium is unimportant to those tiny circuits. To become proficient at machine code it is necessary to have at least a nodding acquaintance with binary although it is certainly not essential to delve into all its ramifications. When first confronted with binary it is a little startling to see strange arithmetic statements like $1 + 1 = 10$ and even worse to learn that $10 + 10 = 100$. However, this will make sense when we memorise the simple progression, 1,2,4,8,16,32,64... etc. and understand that the 'weighting' of any binary digit increases by a power of two from right to left, instead of a power of ten in the familiar decimal system.

Examples:

    11 in binary is a 1 and a 2 in decimal, representing 3.

    101 in binary is a 1 and a 4 in decimal, representing 5.

    1111 in binary is a 1 and a 2 and a 4 and 8, representing 15.

A rather important binary number is 11111111 which you should now be able to translate to 255 in decimal. This number continuously appears in computing manuals and textbooks.

    Addition in binary is exactly the same as in decimal except that a carry to the next column takes place when the *sum exceeds 1* rather than 9.

    Examples are better than wordy descriptions, so spend a few minutes in order to agree that the following makes sense:

$$
\begin{array}{lll}
3 = 0011 & 7 = 0111 & 5 = 0101 \\
+2 = 0010 & +8 = 1000 & +6 = 0110 \\
\hline
5 = 0101 & 15 = 1111 & 11 = 1011 \\
\end{array}
$$

The byte

The meaning of the term *byte* in microcomputing is a string of *eight bits*. A 'bit' (a corruption of <u>BI</u>nary digi<u>T</u>) is a 1 or a 0.

    Why the byte is so important is the fact that most popular machines are, at the moment, 'eight-bit' types. The 6502 is an eight-bit microprocessor, meaning that all transfers of binary data between the memory and the microprocessor take place in blocks of eight bits – the memory is therefore eight bits 'wide'. Each tiny cell in a byte can store a 1 or a 0 so, if the byte is full up (all cells containing 1) the *pure* binary number 11111111 would equal 255 in decimal. You may be wondering why it was necessary to state the word 'pure' binary. This is because there is an alternative way of stating binary bits called *two's complement* in order to cover both positive and negative numbers (see later).

For convenience and clarity, it is customary to consider the byte as if it were made up of two equal 4-bit halves called *nibbles*. The separation has no real significance to the computing circuits.

Hexadecimal notation (hex)

It was necessary to find some quick method of *describing* the contents of a byte. We could, of course, describe it in terms of the decimal equivalent but this is not quick enough. Perhaps you can, but I certainly couldn't, blurt out *instantly* the value of 1011 1101. I could, however, describe it as BD hex almost instantly and probably you will be able to as well – soon.

Hexadecimal is Latin (or maybe Greek) for 'sixteen'. It is a counting system, like binary and decimal, but uses sixteen characters:

0,1,2,3,4,5,6,7,8,9,A,B,C,D,E,F

A nibble is a block of four characters, so there must be 2^4 (sixteen) different combinations of arranging the bits in a nibble. Each combination can be uniquely represented by one hex digit as follows:

Binary	Hex
0000	0
0001	1
0010	2
0011	3
0100	4
0101	5
0110	6
0111	7
1000	8
1001	9
1010	A
1011	B
1100	C
1101	D
1110	E
1111	F

Examples:

1111	1111
F	F

1010	0001
A	1

1000	0000
8	0

1011	0011
B	3

Although used primarily for describing the contents of a byte in terms of a pair of hex digits, we must not forget that it is a legitimate counting system (although a little cumbersome). When adding two hex numbers, a carry is required to the next higher place when the sum exceeds 15 in decimal (F in hex). Care must be taken in intepreting hex in relation to decimal so the following examples may help:

> 10 in hex is 16 in decimal.
> 32 in hex is 50 in decimal.
> 6F in hex is 111 in decimal.
> FFFF in hex is 65 535 in decimal.

To understand these conversions examine the following place weightings of four-hex-digit numbers which progress to the left in increasing powers of 16:

	16^3	16^2	16	1	= (4096	256	16	1)
Example:	0	0	5	F	= $(5 \times 16) + 15 = 95$ decimal
Example:	0	2	D	A	= $(2 \times 256) + (13 \times 16) + 10 =$ 730 decimal
Example:	F	F	F	F	= $(15 \times 4096) + (15 \times 256) + (15 \times 16) + 15 = 65535$

Here are a few examples in the addition of two hex numbers:

$$
\begin{array}{rrrr}
F & FF & AF & ABCD \\
\underline{3} & \underline{01} & \underline{3C} & \underline{0\ 1\ 1\ 1} \\
12 & 100 & EB & ACDE
\end{array}
$$

Manipulations like the above may take some while before they can be carried out instinctively although, fortunately, the majority of hex arithmetic is carried out on one-byte numbers which require only two hex digits. Although the machine code column in an assembly listing always uses hex digits both for the code and operand, the assembly code column is entirely up to you. If you want the operands to be interpreted as hex then you must prefix with '&'. If the prefix is omitted the assembler will assume you mean decimal although, during the internal assembly action, it will be 'silently' converted into binary, via hex, first.

Since you can use decimal at any time, why is it necessary to bother with learning hex? Strange as it may seem, using hex can often be easier than decimal, simply because it is so closely related to binary bits. Until you become convinced of this, however, by all means use only decimal.

Negative numbers and two's complement

A computing system which can deal only with positive numbers would have little use in the real world. In decimal, there is no problem – we just place a '–' before the number to indicate it is negative. But this is out of the question in binary because there are *no other characters* but 0 and 1. Apart from this restriction, there are problems involved with the internal electronic hardware. Inside the microprocessor is a complex area which can *add* numbers together but it cannot perform (or rather has not been designed for) direct subtraction. However, an adding device can be 'persuaded' to subtract by supplying one of the numbers in negative form. The 6502 and, indeed, other common microprocessors use 'two's complement' to represent negative numbers.

Before describing two's complement, it is advisable to understand a few formal definitions used to identify particular bit positions within a byte (see Figure 2.3). The bit at the extreme right of Figure 2.3 is referred to as the lsb (Least Significant Bit). The bit on the extreme left is the msb (Most Significant Bit). Note that the bits are numbered bit-0 to bit-7 for reference purposes so the lsb is bit-0 and the msb is bit 7.

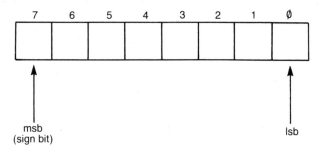

Fig. 2.3. Bit labelling in a byte.

Returning to the case of negative numbers, these can be identified by the msb. This qualifies the msb for the additional title of *sign bit*.

A negative number has a 1 in the msb position.

Thus, 0110 1101 is a positive number but 1010 1110 is a negative number. Since 0000 0010 is clearly how +2 would be held, it may come as a shock to learn that −2 is held as 1111 1110. The sign bit is certainly a 1 but why are there so many other positions with a 1 in them? This is the fault of the microprocessor designed for two's complement. The rule to find the equivalent negative numbers is:

> To find the equivalent negative of a binary number, change every bit of the equivalent positive and then add 1.

Here is how +2 can be changed to −2, using the above rule:

$$0000\ 0010 \quad \text{is} +2$$
Change the bits: 1111 1101
Now add 1: 1111 1110   is −2

Note that in hex, +2 is 02 but −2 is FE. If the process of adding the the extra 1 causes a carry to propagate through and 'drop' out at the msb end, it doesn't matter and can be ignored. There is an alternative and less error-prone method of finding the negative:

> As an alternative method, to find the negative equivalent of a positive binary number, start from the right and copy down up to and including the first 1. Thereafter, change every bit.

Examples:

+2 = 0000 0010	+1 = 0000 0001	+127 = 0111 1111
−2 = 1111 1110	−1 = 1111 1111	−127 = 1000 0001
In hex terms, +2 = 02	+1 = 01	+127 = 7F
−2 = FE	−1 = FF	−127 = 81

Maximum capacity of one byte

It is clear from the above that a single byte is limited in the size of numbers it can handle. It is worth memorising the following:

The largest positive number in one byte is 7F hex (+127 decimal).
The largest negative number in one byte is 80 hex (−128 decimal).
The largest number in *unsigned-binary* is FF hex (255 decimal).

The term *unsigned-binary* is used when negative numbers are not catered for, in which case the msb is not 'wasted'.

If larger numbers than the above have to be handled it is necessary to reserve more than one byte per number. The programmer must imagine that the separate bytes are joined end to end with only the most significant byte acting as the sign bit (see Figure 2.4).

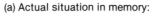

(a) Actual situation in memory:

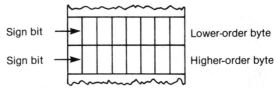

(b) As visualised by the programmer:

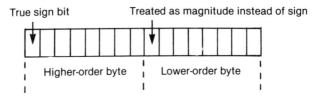

Fig. 2.4.   Storing double-byte signed numbers.

Example:
   0111 1111   1111 1111 would be +32,767 in decimal
   (7FFF hex)

Employing more than one byte number is called *multi-precision* and must be organised by the programmer; the 6502 will have no idea what you are supposed to be doing. As far as the 6502 is concerned it knows it is an 8-bit micro and is unconcerned (perhaps even slightly amused) at the human's awkward attempts to enlarge its girth! One advantage of the new 16-bit microprocessors is the ability to handle larger numbers without using multi-precision techniques. Multi-precision, using two 16-bit registers or memory cells, would handle two's complement numbers in the range of plus or minus 2000 million. If you can tolerate yet another formula, the following is a quick way to discover the largest positive number:

> The largest positive number in a set of N bits is $2^{N-1}-1$
> (where N is the number of bits).

Examples:
With 8 bits, this becomes $2^7 - 1 = 127$
With 16 bits, $2^{15} - 1 = 32767$
With 32 bits, $2^{31} - 1 = 2147483653$

The largest negative number is always *one more* than the equivalent positive. Justification for this rather startling snippet is due to the convention that zero is a positive number and therefore a passenger. (See Figure 2.5 for the circular nature of two's complement.)

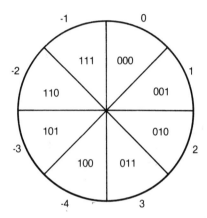

Fig. 2.5. Visualising two's complement numbers. (For simplicity a three-bit word is used.)

Summary

- Analogue computers *measure*. Digital computers *count*.
- A *bit* is a 1 or a 0, a *nibble* is four bits and a *byte* is eight bits.
- The binary counting system is based on powers of *two* instead of ten so each binary bit is worth double the value of the bit on its right.
- The contents of a byte can be described easily by two hex digits.
- The hexadecimal counting system is based on powers of sixteen so each hex digit is worth sixteen times the value of the digit on its right.
- *Numbers* in assembly code are interpreted as decimal unless prefixed by '&', in which case they are assumed to be hex.
- Numbers of either sign can be represented in *two's complement* form.
- If the extreme left-hand bit (the msb) is a 1, the number is treated by the microprocessor circuits as negative.
- It is conventional to identify each bit by numbering them bit 0 to bit 7 – bit 0 being the lsb and bit 7 the msb.

- The largest positive number in a byte is +127 and the largest negative is-128.
- Two or more bytes considered end to end can represent larger numbers although this technique is a software dodge. It is not hardware implemented.
- If the msb is not considered by the programmer as a sign bit, the number is said to be in *unsigned binary* and raises the maximum absolute number in a byte to 255 decimal (FF hex).

Chapter Three
Registers, Transfers and Arithmetic

It is never easy to decide how much detail should be written on the technicalities of the microprocessor. It is possible to understand machine code and compose useful programs without wading through masses of Silicon Valley jargon. On the other hand, it is certainly advisable to cultivate a mild curiosity. It is absolutely necessary to be aware of the various registers in the 6502 which are programmable but whether or not it is equally necessary to study the other bits and pieces is open to question. The trouble with microprocessors is the mind-bending complexity of their electronic intestines. Even a superficial attempt to unravel the timing sequences alone would take many pages of difficult text and almost certainly dissuade many readers from progressing further. Consequently, this chapter will be based on the 'need to know' philosophy rather than attempt an over-simplified treatment which would be of little real assistance.

The internal registers

A *register* is similar to a normal memory location in RAM, in that it can hold a string of eight bits (one byte). It differs in two ways; it is inside the microprocessor chip and capable of more sophisticated action than a RAM location. The most important register of all is the *program counter* but, because it is mainly automatic in action rather than directly programmable, is not of much interest to us at this stage. The most important registers for our present purpose are the *accumulator*, the *X-register* and the *Y-register* (see Figure 3.1). During the course of a program, one or more of these will be holding data or modifying it in some way. There will be a continuous interchange of data between these registers and the memory system external to the microprocessor. It would appear, from a superficial

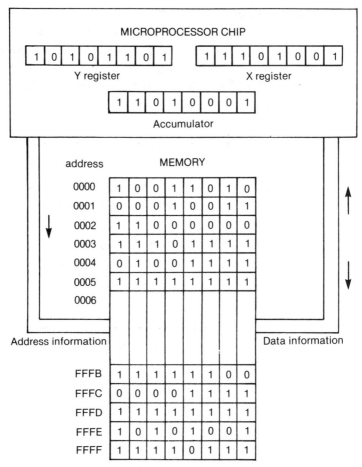

Fig. 3.1. Programmer's view of the registers A, X, Y and memory. (Contents of registers and memory are fictitious.)

glance at some of the assembly listings which appear in magazines and books, that machine code programming consists of pointless transfers of data from one register to another then back again – rushing back and forth getting nowhere! This impression is excusable if you are unfamiliar with the limitations imposed on some of the registers. The following is a brief outline of the capabilities of each register:

(a) *The accumulator* (referred to as 'A')

This is the most powerful and consequently the most overworked register in the microprocessor. It is the only register with true arithmetic capabilities but, even so, only addition and subtraction are possible. Its contents can be transferred to any other register or to memory.

(b) *The X-register* (referred to as 'X')
This register cannot perform addition or subtraction. It can, however, be *incremented* (increased by 1) or *decremented* (decreased by 1). Transfers to other registers and memory are possible. It is also used for a special kind of addressing known as *indexed-addressing*.

(c) *The Y-register* (referred to as 'Y')
The Y-register is similar to the X-register in nearly every respect and is also used for indexed addressing.

Table 1 shows the assembly op-codes of register operations and the corresponding actions. The reference to *stack-pointer* is anticipating later discussion.

Table 1.   Simple register operations.

Mnemonic op-code	Action
TAX	Transfer contents of A to X
TXA	Transfer contents of X to A
TAY	Transfer contents of A to Y
TYA	Transfer contents of Y to A
INX	Increment contents of X
DEX	Decrement contents of X
INY	Increment contents of Y
DEY	Decrement contents of Y
TXS	Transfer contents of X to stack-pointer
TSX	Transfer contents of stack-pointer to X

It is important to understand the rather specialised computer meaning of the term *transfer*. When, for example, the action is described as: 'Transfer contents of A to X', it means a *copy* of the contents of A is transferred to X. The contents of A remain the same but the original contents of X are over-written by the transfer action. It is worth emphasising this with an example:

Suppose A contains 52 and X contains 67 now. After TAX, X will contain 52 and A will still have 52.

The operations defined in Table 1 have one common attribute in that they are *complete* instructions to the 6502. They require no operand because the op-code itself tells the system all it needs to know. The jargon term for this *implied addressing* and is clearly an efficient programming weapon. Refer back to Example 1.1 of Chapter One to confirm that, apart from RTS, none of the assembly instructions have used implied addressing – they all required an operand of some sort.

Example 3.1 performs the same objective (displays the characters 'ABC' at the centre of the screen) but is re-arranged in order to illustrate implied addressing. The revised program saves two bytes and only uses one register. Not perhaps an exciting improvement, but the intention was to illustrate implied addressing.

```
 10 REM *EXAMPLE 3.1*
 20 MODE 7:CLS
 30 P%=&D00:REM SET PROG COUNTER
 35 Screen=32320
 40 [
 50 LDX #65 \ ASCII for'A'
 60 STX Screen
 70 INX
 80 STX Screen+1
 90 INX
100 STX Screen+2
110 RTS
120 ]
130 END
```

Example 3.1. Using implied addressing.

The INX lines modify the ASCII code to produce 'B' and 'C'.

Clearing registers and memory locations

It is often required to set a register to 0000 0000 (00 hex). Some microprocessors have special op-codes to 'clear' the accumulator or other registers such as CLA,CLX,CLY etc., but the 6502 is a little mean in this respect. If a register is to be set to zero (cleared) it must be done by setting the number zero into the register by using *immediate addressing*. Example 3.2 illustrates the clearing of all three registers and one memory location – just for luck.

The accumulator has been cleared first by LDA #0. The X and Y registers have been cleared by transfers from the accumulator and, finally, the address 32320 (centre of screen) is cleared by forcing the accumulator data into it.

```
  10 REM *EXAMPLE 3.2 CLEARING*
  20 MODE 7:CLS
  30 P%=&D00
  35 Screen=32320
  40 [
  50 LDA #0
  60 TAX
  70 TAY
  80 STA 32320
  90 NOP
 100 NOP
 110 RTS
 120 ]
 130 END

>RUN
0D00
0D00 A9 00      LDA #0
0D02 AA         TAX
0D03 A8         TAY
0D04 8D 40 7E   STA 32320
0D07 EA         NOP
0D08 EA         NOP
0D09 60         RTS
```

Example 3.2. Clearing registers and use of NOP.

Note that two, previously undefined 'NOPs' have been slipped in at lines 90 and 100. NOP means No OPeration and it certainly lives up to its name because it literally *does nothing*. The obvious question is 'Why use the stupid thing?' Strangely enough, there are times when it is useful, particularly during program development because it provides a temporary and tidy breathing space which can be exchanged for a useful operation at any time. In our example, it merely occupies two line numbers which were formerly occupied in the previous examples. All examples up to now have been fitted into lines 40 to 120 as far as the assembly code is concerned – for no reason other than consistency. NOPs are also useful for 'fine-tuning' a timing loop – it takes time even to do nothing!

Addition and subtraction

There are only two arithmetical operations possible with the 6502, ADC, which means 'ADd with Carry' and SBC, which means

'SuBtract with Carry'. Forgetting the reference to 'carry' for the moment, ADC and SBC can add or subtract any mixture of positive and negative numbers. That is to say, ADC can add 3 to 5, 3 to −5, −3 to −5 etc. SBC has similar flexibility. But, and it is a big but, there is a miserably low limit to the size of numbers which can be handled. In BASIC, we tend to be spoon-fed and take enormous numbers for granted, thinking perhaps the 'computer' is clever enough to take such numbers in its stride. In reality, the poor old 6502 microprocessor (and indeed most other 8-bit types) fails to handle two's complement numbers greater than +127 or −128. You will remember this limitation was discussed in the previous chapter. It is the intellect and craftiness of human programmers which give the computer its apparent arithmetical dexterity. It is system programmers which fool the microprocessor into performing multiplication, division, sines and cosines, etc. Returning now to the subject of our primitive ADC and SBC, it is time we set out a formal definition, including the use of the 'carry bit'.

Table 2. Addition and subtraction.

Mnemonic op-code	Action
ADC	Add the number, as defined by the operand, to the existing contents of the accumulator. Any carry is taken into consideration.
SBC	Subtract the number, as defined by the operand, from the existing contents of the accumulator. Any carry is taken into consideration.
CLC	Clear the carry bit. (Make it 0.)
SEC	Set the carry bit. (Make it 1.)
CLV	Clear the overflow bit. (Make it 0.)
INC	Increment contents of memory.
DEC	Decrement contents of memory.

Note from Table 2 that the result is *always* in the accumulator. The phrase 'as defined by the operand' may seem a bit frightening but is necessary in a formal definition. Remember, the *operand* is that part of the instruction which follows the op-code. The *meaning* of the operand, however, depends on the *addressing mode*. The 6502 is a very 'powerful' species of microprocessor, due mainly to the rich variety of addressing modes available. Some of the modes are fiendish in their subtlety and will not be attempted in this book.

Up to the present, the addressing modes encountered have been:

(a) *Implied addressing*, in which no operand is necessary.

(b) *Immediate addressing*, in which the operand is the *actual data*. The assembler recognises this mode by the prefix #.

(c) *Absolute addressing*, in which the operand is the address at which the data is stored.

```
10 REM *EXAMPLE 3.3 ADDING*
20 MODE 7:CLS
30 P%=&D00
40 [
50 CLC
60 LDA #24
70 STA &0DFF
80 LDA #32
90 ADC &0DFF
100 STA &0DFE
110 RTS
120 ]
130 CALL&0D00
140 PRINT"Accumulator contains ";?&0DFE
150 END

>RUN
0D00
0D00 18          CLC
0D01 A9 18       LDA #24
0D03 8D FF 0D    STA &0DFF
0D06 A9 20       LDA #32
0D08 6D FF 0D    ADC &0DFF
0D0B 8D FE 0D    STA &0DFE
0D0E 60          RTS
Accumulator contains 56
```

Example 3.3.   Addition of numbers.

It would be as well to glance back at Example 3.2 to confirm the symbols for the addressing modes. Thus line 50 is an example of *immediate* addressing because of the #. The data is 0. Line 60 is *implied* addressing because there is no operand. Line 80 is *absolute* addressing because it refers not to the actual data but the address in memory *where* the data is to be placed.

We return now to a simple program to illustrate addition (see Example 3.3). The program adds 24 and 32 together and stores the result in address &0DFE which is subsequently printed out by the BASIC statement ?&0DFE in line 140. In most other machines, this would be a PEEK instruction but the equivalent in BBC BASIC is by using the '?' operator (see page 409 in the *User Guide*). The first number, 24, is placed in the accumulator using immediate addressing and is then stored temporarily at the bottom end of our safe area using absolute addressing. The second number, 32, is now placed in the accumulator, overwriting the previous contents. The original number, stored in &0DFF is then *added* to the accumulator using ADC with absolute addressing (line 90). The result is then stored in another safe area, &0DFE, before returning to BASIC.

The program claims no merit with regard to efficiency or memory economy. These points have been ignored in order to illustrate the addressing modes previously discussed. For example, there was no need to waste two memory locations in the safe area because the result could have been stored back in the original &0DFF. Valid criticism could also be directed at the use of immediate addressing for the two numbers. The program can only act on the two *constants* 24 and 32; consequently the only way to add two other numbers would be to alter the operands in lines 60 and 80. But then it could also be argued that the program is silly anyway – all this messing around just to add a couple of numbers which would be child's play in BASIC!

A well-known platitude states that 'you can't run before you can walk'. When you first attempt to learn machine code a more pertinent version would be 'you can't walk until you can crawl'. This is the first and only apology I make for subsequent programs which may appear too low-brow for high-brow readers.

There remains one line in the example unexplained – the CLC in line 50. When any program or segment of a program uses ADC it is essential that the 'carry-bit', which may have been left over from a previous arithmetic bout, is rendered harmless. Before the details can be discussed we must find out a little more about this carry-bit.

The carry-bit (C)

We must first establish where this mysterious C-bit lives. Apart from the accumulator, X- and Y-registers, there is another register within the microprocessor called the Process Status Register (PSR). Unlike the three registers previously described, it is a hotchpotch of entirely unrelated *flag-bits*. The term *flag-bit* is used to describe a single bit which, depending on whether it is a 1 or a 0, signals that some condition is true or false – something has happened or not happened. When certain of the op-codes are executed, one of the bits in the PSR called the C-bit is *automatically* set to 1 if the operation has resulted in a 1 being pushed out at the left-hand end of the 'destination' register. Instead of this bit 'falling on the floor' it is popped into the C-bit position in the PSR. The C-bit may be thought of as the ninth bit of the other registers. It is this bit, and the other flag bits in the PSR, which decide the course of events which follow conditional branch type instructions. These are not dealt with until later.

Our main concern at the moment is its effect on the ADC instruction. Suppose we use ADC to add, say, 3 to 5 and by chance the C-bit contained a 1, left as residue from a previous operation. Since it is taken into consideration during an ADC action (refer back to Table 2) it would make the answer 9 instead of 8. For this reason, it is prudent always to clear it with CLC before using ADC. Some microprocessors have two 'add' type instructions. One is a normal ADD which ignores the C-bit and the other is an ADC which doesn't. The 6502, however, is not favoured in this direction so the onus of clearing the flag is always the responsibility of the machine code programmer. My follow-up book to this one, *Get More From BBC Micro Machine Code* (Granada) includes examples of multi-precision addition or subtraction where it will be apparent how useful the C-bit is for 'joining' two registers end to end in order to handle larger numbers.

To try out the effect of the C-bit, change line 50 in Example 3.3 from CLC to SEC which pushes a 1 directly into the flag. When you re-run the program again, the answer will be one too many.

The overflow-bit (the V-bit)

The other flag bit in the PSR associated with arithmetic operations is concerned with detecting an overflow condition. If, as the result of using ADC or SBC, the result is invalid from a two's complement arithmetic viewpoint, due to the result being too large for the register to handle, the *V-bit* is automatically set. This can subsequently be tested for by one of the conditional branch instructions.

It may seem puzzling to some what exactly is the difference between a carry-out condition and overflow. If there is a carry-out, there must also be an overflow condition – surely? From a common-sense viewpoint this is true but arithmetic circuits in microprocessors do not work on common-sense – and a good thing too, because humans would not always agree on what is a particular 'common-sense' interpretation.

Without plunging into a dry discourse on the ramifications of two's complement arithmetic it may be accepted at this point that it is possible to have an overflow condition *without a carry-out*. Conversely, it is equally possible to have a carry-out with no overflow so it is necessary for the PSR to have both a C-bit and a V-bit to distinguish the computer status at any time. When we deal with branch instructions it will be seen that the C and V bits can be tested to establish a wide variety of conditions besides addition and subtraction.

Subtraction

To examine the SBC facility, two changes are required to Example 3.3. Obviously, line 90 must be changed from ADC to SBC but it may come as a mild shock to discover that line 50 must also be changed from CLC to SEC. It is yet another infuriating quirk of two's complement arithmetic that the carry-bit must be set to 1 before performing subtraction. The reason for this is due to the back-handed way subtraction is performed. The micro circuits use the same *adding* circuitry to subtract, relying on the mathematical dodge that 'adding the negative' is the same as subtraction. Because the 'negative' is formed by changing all the bits from 0 to 1 (and *vice versa*) then the carry bit must also suffer the same fate.

Using the in-built subroutines

It is understandable if the previous description of simple arithmetic leaves you with the impression that it is all too fiddly and error-prone to bother with. However, before you sigh wearily and rush back to BASIC there is a bright patch – you really needn't bother too much about all this detail. One of the valuable features of the BBC assembler is the ease with which the subroutines, already resident in the ROM, can be called up in your machine code. It is impossible to compete with the professionally written subroutines for the handling of arithmetic and mathematical functions. Acorn have been generous in allowing easy access to their internal software and, instead of the usual cloud of secrecy practised by some other manufacturers, openly encourage you to utilise them by giving the starting addresses and instructions on their use. Also, it is possible to mix complex operations normal to BASIC with machine code and we shall be illustrating some of these useful aids later.

There is one snag, however, with the over-use of these pre-written subroutines when you are learning machine code for the first time. If, for example, you write a program which produces flashly pictures on the screen in 'machine code' by simply stringing together other people's subroutines, can you really say to your friends: 'Look what I've done with machine code'? Apart from matters of conscience, it is as well to think hard about your objectives. I think the best advice is to learn the basic elements of machine code a bit at a time, mixing in some pre-written subroutines whenever you are stuck or when the need for the program is more important than the methods used to write it. There is one question worth answering regarding over-dependence on pre-written subroutines: 'What happens if there is no subroutine which fits your particular requirements?'

X- and Y-register arithmetic

As mentioned before, the accumulator is the only register that can make use of the add and subtract instructions. If numbers are to be added or subtracted from, say, the X-register then a choice of two courses is open to you:

(a) Transfer from X to A, perform the arithmetic and transfer the result back to X.
(b) Perform a series of separate increments (using INX) or separate decrements (using DEX).

To add small numbers less than, say, five, method (b) can be used although it must be admitted that too many consecutive INX lines do have an amateurish appearance.

Method (a) can be used with any numbers, providing they are within the previously defined limits. There is, however, a pitfall which can cause unexpected corruption of data. It is highly probable that the existing contents of the accumulator are important, so the act of using it as an intermediary for the X-register arithmetic will certainly play havoc with the contents. The only way out would be a temporary storage of the accumulator contents into a memory location whilst the X-register transfers take place. It is evident from this short dissertation on the possible perils that a considerable amount of care must be taken, even when the objective is a simple addition. There is one brilliant little dodge, provided by the 6502, for taking care of temporary storage of the accumulator contents without bothering to trouble about any particular memory address. This useful piece of hardware is called the *stack*.

```
 10 REM *EXAMPLE 3.4 THE STACK*
 20 MODE 7:CLS
 30 P%=&D00
 40 [
 50 CLC              \Clear C-bit
 60 LDA #65          \ASCII for A
 70 PHA              \Push Acc
 80 ADC #3           \Add 3
 90 STA 32320        \Print to screen
100 PLA              \Pull Acc
110 STA 32322        \Print to screen
120 RTS
130 ]
140 END

>RUN
0D00
0D00 18          CLC            \Clear C-bit
0D01 A9 41       LDA #65        \ASCII for A
0D03 48          PHA            \Push Acc
0D04 69 03       ADC #3         \Add 3
0D06 8D 40 7E    STA 32320      \Print to screen
0D09 68          PLA            \Pull Acc
0D0A 8D 42 7E    STA 32322      \Print to screen
0D0D 60          RTS

>CALL&0D00
```

Example 3.4. Using the stack.

The stack

What use is the stack? The short answer is to provide a handy, no-nonsense dumping ground for the accumulator. It is not proposed to deal intimately with the sordid details of the thing at this stage. Instead, just let's use it.

Suppose you want temporarily to store the accumulator contents while it is used to help out the X- or Y-register. All you have to do is write PHA. This will push the accumulator contents on to the stack (PHA is the mnemonic op-code for PusH Accumulator). When you are ready to put it back use PLA. This means PulL Accumulator. Note there is no operand required because the stack is the implied address. Example 3.4 shows a simple stack operation.

The remarks on the listing explain what is happening but a few words may help to explain why the result, after CALL&0D00, is 'D A' on the screen. If you study the code carefully you will be satisfied that the stack has done its job. The original accumulator contained the ASCII for A but the last contents became ASCII for D. The fact that D appears, then A, confirms that the Push and Pull did their job properly. Although only the accumulator is involved, it is of course possible to push X or Y onto the stack *via* the accumulator, by the use of TXA and TYA. There are times when it may be necessary to push the contents of the PSR onto the stack and this can be done directly by the use of PHP and recalled by PLP.

The four stack op-codes are collected together in Table 3.

Table 3.   Stack operations.

Mnemonic op-code	Action
PHA	Push Accumulator onto stack
PLA	Pull Accumulator from stack
PHP	Push Process Status Register (PSR) onto stack
PLP	Pull PSR from stack

The stack can be used without knowing all the details of the rather complex hardware behind it. There is one aspect, however, which is of paramount importance – it behaves as a Last In First Out (LIFO) memory. This means you can keep pushing data onto the stack, one on top of the other like a pile of dinner plates. But, you can only retrieve them in the inverse order. The last dinner plate on the pile must be the first to be taken off in most sensible kitchens. Thus, if you wish to store all registers on the stack, say, in the order A then X then Y then PSR, you must retrieve them in the order PSR then Y then X and finally A. The computer will give you no help in this matter and it will be up to you to keep track of the order of retrieval. The microprocessor employs a special device called the *stack pointer* (SP) to organise the stack addresses, although it is unnecessary to worry too much about it at this stage.

Example 3.5 shows one way of pushing all the registers onto the stack.

```
10 REM *EXAMPLE 3.5 Stack all*
20 MODE 7:CLS
30 P%=&D00
40 [
50 PSHA           \Push Acc
60 TXA
70 PSHA           \Push X
80 TYA
90 PSHA           \Push Y
100 PHP           \Push PSR
110 RTS
120 ]
130 END
```

Example 3.5. Saving registers on the stack.

It should be emphasised that storing on the stack is both convenient and economical in memory space because there is *no* operand required. There is a limit to the amount of data which can be stored. If the stack is caused to 'rise' too much without periodic 'falls' (too many pushes and not enough pulls) there is a danger of overflow. Unlike BASIC, the assembler doesn't always offer kindly warnings so it is possible for stack overflow to occur without knowing it except, of course, the difficulty of locating the bug.

Register/memory transfers

Although the X and Y registers cannot use the stack directly, they can be stored anywhere in memory and loaded back. Table 4 is the collection of op-codes applicable, including the accumulator transfers.

Table 4. Register/memory transfers.

Mnemonic op-codes	Action
LDA	Load the data, as defined by the operand, into the accumulator
STA	Store the accumulator contents in memory as defined by the operand
LDX	Load the data, as defined by the operand, into the X-register
STX	Store the X-register contents in memory as defined by the operand
LDY	Load the data, as defined by the operand, into the Y-register
STY	Store the Y-register contents in memory as defined by the operand

As explained earlier in the discussion on register to register transfers, there is no actual transfer of data from 'source' to 'destination'. Only a *copy* of the source data is transferred. The rule can be stated concisely in the following terms:

> The data at the *source* still remains intact.
> The original contents at the *destination* is replaced by the new data.

The above rule is worth an example:

Suppose X contains 34 and address &0DFF contains 56. After LDX &0DFF, X will contain 56 and so will address &0DFF.

Page zero addressing
If the address is within the range &0000 to &00FF, although still an 'absolute' address in the academic sense, it is sub-classified as *page zero*. The two leading zeros can be dropped allowing the operand to be expressed in only two hex digits. Page zero addressing is economical but, unfortunately, most of it is utilised by the operating system.

Summary

- A *register* is an 8-bit storage device like any memory location but is situated *within* the microprocessor and has a more sophisticated action.
- The accumulator is the most important general purpose register and the most sophisticated.
- The X-register and the Y-register can be used for general purpose transfers, can be incremented, decremented and are fundamental to the process of *indexed addressing.*
- Whenever data is transferred from source to destination, the source data is retained but the original destination data is overwritten.
- All instructions have an op-code but not all have an operand.
- Op-codes which require no operand rely on *implied addressing.*
- If the operand is prefixed by #, it is using *immediate addressing* because the operand *is* the data.
- If the operand is not prefixed by # it is called *absolute addressing* and is the address at which the data is to be found.
- Addresses can be assumed to be decimal unless the operand is prefixed by &, in which case they are assumed to be hexadecimal.
- Addition and subtraction can only be carried out with the accumulator, the result always being left in the accumulator.
- Addition uses ADC, which takes into consideration the C-bit. Subtraction uses SBC and also takes into consideration the C-bit.
- The C-bit is situated within the microprocessor register called the Process Status Register (PSR) and is set to 1 automatically when a carry occurs.
- The C-bit should be cleared by CLC before commencing an addition.
- The C-bit should be set to 1 by SEC before commencing a subtraction.
- The V-bit in the PSR is set to 1 automatically if the result is too large to be contained in a register.
- The stack is a last-in-first-out memory, useful for the temporary dumping of a register content.
- Data pushed onto the stack must be retrieved in inverse order.

Chapter Four
Branching, Comparisons and Subroutines

A microprocessor executes all instructions in strict address order unless it comes across a 'jump' or 'branch-if' op-code. In BASIC, of course, there is the dreaded GOTO (virtually outlawed by the exponents of structured programming) and the IF/THEN statements. The ease with which these can be incorporated in programs disguises the quite difficult machine code which they make use of. Without the help given by the BBC assembler, branch instructions would become a nightmare. Table 5 defines the BRANCH type of instructions.

Table 5. Conditional branching.

Mnemonic op-codes	Action
BNE	Branch if Not Equal to operand destination
BEQ	Branch if Equal to operand destination
BPL	Branch if Plus (if positive) to operand destination
BMI	Branch if Minus (if negative) to operand destination
BCC	Branch if Carry Clear to operand destination
BCS	Branch if Carry Set to operand destination
BVC	Branch if Overflow Clear to operand destination
BVS	Branch if Overflow Set to operand destination

The action column descriptions clearly call for some additional explanation. We will pick one of the most commonly used branches as an example, BNE. There are two problems:

(a) *Precise meaning of the op-code BNE*
It is all very well to say 'Branch if not equal' but it poses the question

'Branch if *what* is not equal?'. The answer is simply the result of the *previous* operation. Only if this was *non-zero*, will the branch take place. If zero, the normal sequential address rhythm continues.

(b) *Significance of the operand*

If the branch conditions are met, the operand informs the system where to branch to. That is to say, at what address the next instruction lies. In common with operands of previously discussed op-codes, the operand can be an actual address although, in the case of branch instructions, disguised in a strange form called *relative* addressing. Fortunately we can, with no great loss of continuity in this book, skip the depressing details of relative addressing and go straight on to symbolic address *labels*. The operand is then a name of your own choice, telling the system to *find a line labelled by this name*. The label, which marks the destination line, must begin with a full-stop (or 'period' as it is called in America).

The following plan may help:

```
BNE GRANADA
other instructions
.GRANADA STA &0DFE
```

If the branch conditions are met (the previous operation resulted in zero), the control passes to the line labelled GRANADA. Be very careful not to miss the full-stop in the destination line and ensure there is one space between the end of the label and the beginning of the op-code (STA is purely an example and could be any other op-code).

The importance of the PSR

We had a cursory introduction to the PSR when dealing with the C-bit and the V-bit. Because the branch instructions rely heavily on the bits in this register, the time has come to delve a little deeper into its private parts. Figure 4.1 shows the various bits and their respective positions within the PSR.

After nearly every instruction except branch instructions, the relevant bits in the PSR are up-dated. When a branch instruction is encountered, it is the appropriate bit in the PSR which is 'consulted' before the machine decides to branch or not branch. Thus, if the last instruction resulted in a negative number, the N-bit would have been

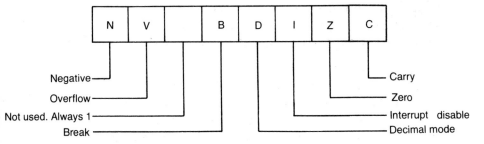

Fig.4.1. The Process Status Register (PSR).

set. On the other hand, if the result was a positive number, the N-bit would have been reset.

Suppose, for example, we use the branch code BPL (which is branch if plus). The machine will examine the N-bit in the PSR and will only take the branch if it is 0. In other words, it is *not-negative*! It is worth mentioning again here that zero is a positive number (see also Chapter Three). Forgetting this is a common cause of teeth-gnashing due to a loop behaving unpredictably. If we use BNE (branch if not equal), the branch will take place only if the Z-bit is 0.

```
 10 REM *EXAMP 4.1 BNE BRANCH*
 20 MODE 7:CLS
 30 P%=&0D00
 40 [
 50      LDX #255
 60 .BACK DEX
 70      BNE BACK
 80      RTS
 90 ]
100 END

>RUN
0D00
0D00 A2 FF    LDX #255
0D02 CA       .BACK DEX
0D03 D0 FD    BNE BACK
0D05 60       RTS
```

Example 4.1. Single loop delay.

It should be emphasised that the PSR bits (with the exception of the D and I bits) are *automatically* set or reset every time an instruction is executed, irrespective of whether it is a branch instruction. In fact, the actual branch instructions are unusual in that they themselves *do not* up-date the PSR bits; they only act upon their advice.

Example 4.1 is an example of a simple loop to illustrate the BNE op-code. The number 255, the largest which can be held in a single byte, is set into X and counted down (decremented by DEX) until it is 'empty'. Note the label BACK, which is the destination of the BNE branch each time round. It could be used as a *delay* subroutine although the actual delay would be of the order of a millisecond. Both BNE and DEX both take two 'clock' cycles. The clock frequency in the BBC machine is 2 million cycles per second (2 MHz) so the time for each cycle is 1/(2 million) which is half a microsecond. To finish the 256 revolutions of the loop will take 128 microseconds.

With an assembler, the machine code equivalent can remain a merciful mystery but it is worth the occasional glance, if only for mental stimulation. Take a look at the assembly listing of Example 4.1 and compare the machine code with the equivalent assembly on the right. Note that LDX 255 has been assembled to A2 FF. The 'A2' part is the machine code for LDX (using immediate addressing) and the operand FF is the hex for 255 decimal. The next line DEX is assembled to CA and the label BACK has vanished from the machine code. This is because 'labels' are not part of machine code, merely an assembler artifice for the convenience of the programmer. How much of a convenience this can be is vividly illustrated in the BNE BACK line which is assembled to D0 FD. The 'D0' part is easy; the machine code for BNE. But why is the operand FD? It is because the intention is to branch *three bytes back* (−3). In two's complement binary, (−3) decimal is 1111 1101 or FD hex. It was mentioned previously that the branch instructions use 'relative' addressing which means relative to the present address. However, it is a relief to know that the BBC assembler is kind enough to take on this messy operation – all you have to do is to decide the name of the label!

Two-pass assembly

The previous examples required *one pass* only through the assembler. Thus, when we typed RUN, the system has been able to assemble your instructions into machine code. Even the last example, including the branch label, was sorted out successfully because the label was encountered *before* the branch instruction.

However, if the program is such that a branch instruction refers to a label which has not yet been encountered, the assembly fails. The first time the assembly is initiated, the label is noted and 'remembered'. If it was passed through the second time the previous label is found and the assembly is valid.

In general, it is advisable to force two passes for all programs which contain branching labels. The method for implementing the double-pass has become 'standardised' to a FOR/NEXT loop. Example 4.2 shows the method and also a few branches to work out.

```
 10 REM *EXAMPLE 4.2 TWO PASSES*
 20 MODE 7:CLS
 30 SCREEN=32320
 32 REM_____
 40 FOR PASS=0 TO 3 STEP 3
 50 P%=&0D00
 60 [
 70 OPT PASS
 80     LDX #80    \ASCII FOR 'P'
 90     LDY #78    \ASCII FOR 'N'
100     LDA #127   \TEST NUMBER
110     BMI NEG
120     STX SCREEN
130     RTS
140.NEG STY SCREEN
150 RTS
160 ]
170 NEXT
172 REM_____
180 CALL &0D00

>RUN
0D00
0D00
0D00              OPT PASS
0D00 A2 50     LDX #80    \ASCII FOR 'P'
0D02 A0 4E     LDY #78    \ASCII FOR 'N'
0D04 A9 7F     LDA #127   \TEST NUMBER
0D06 30 04     BMI NEG
0D08 8E 40 7E  STX SCREEN
0D0B 60        RTS
0D0C 8C 40 7E  .NEG STY SCREEN
0D0F 60        RTS
```

Example 4.2. Two-pass assembly.

The object of the program is to print out P on the screen if the 'test' number is positive, but N if it is negative. The test number is at line 100 and is fixed at 127. You will remember that this is the highest number in two's complement arithmetic recognised as 'positive' 7F in hex. When the program is RUN the character 'P' appears as we should expect. It is a valuable exercise to alter the number a few times. If you try any number between 128 and 255 (7F to FF hex) the character 'N' should appear.

So much for the object, which is the simple part. The next obstacle is the two-pass action of the FOR/NEXT. During the first pass, the assembly is under OPT 0 which, as explained in Chapter 1, stops the assembly listing and any error reports. The second pass is under OPT 3 which gives the listing and errors (if any). The part within the FOR loop is demarcated by dotted lines to emphasise the bits and pieces which *must* be enclosed in future programs requiring two-passes. Note particularly that the program counter assignment (P%) must be within the loop and OPT must be within the square bracket area.

The next example (Example 4.3) is concerned with the overflow test BVS. It also shows how variables from the BASIC area can be passed to the assembler. There are more efficient ways of doing this but it is wise to progress gradually from the familiar to the unfamiliar.

The objective is to add two numbers, both of which can be passed from BASIC, and test for the overflow condition. A secondary objective is to provide practice in the interpretation of two's complement numbers. Instead of the test numbers being embedded as constants, the operands in lines 140 and 150 are symbolic names, passed from INPUT statements. The numbers you decide to enter may result in assembly error messages which provide training material. Some typical results are as follows:

(a) *Numbers entered greater than 255 decimal*
If either of the numbers entered exceed 255 decimal, the error message will be 'BYTE AT LINE 140' (or line 150) as appropriate. This is because the assembler cannot place such numbers into a single byte register.

(b) *Numbers entered with a negative sign such as −34*
A negative sign is quite intelligible to us but a microprocessor is 'trained' on two's complement arithmetic for negative numbers and fails to recognise '−'. A similar error message as in (a) above is displayed.

```
10 REM *EXAMPLE 4.3 OVERFLOW*
20 MODE 7:CLS
30 SCREEN=32520
40 INPUT"Enter number "First_number
50 INPUT"Enter another number "Second_number
60 REM_____
70 FOR PASS=0 TO 3 STEP 3
80 P%=&0D00
90 [
100 OPT PASS
110     CLV
120     LDX #83     \ASCII for'S'
130     LDY #86     \ASCII for'V'
140     LDA #First_number
150     ADC #Second_number
160     BVS OVF
170     STX SCREEN         STA &0DFF
180     RTS
190.OVF STY SCREEN
200     RTS
210 ]
220 NEXT      PRINT "Accumulator contains"; ?&0DFF
230 REM_____
240 CALL &0D00
>RUN
Enter number 127
Enter another number 2
0D00
0D00
0D00            OPT PASS
0D00 B8         CLV
0D01 A2 53      LDX #83     \ASCII for'S'
0D03 A0 56      LDY #86     \ASCII for'V'
0D05 A9 7F      LDA #First_number
0D07 69 02      ADC #Second_number
0D09 70 04      BVS OVF
0D0B 8E 08 7F   STX SCREEN
0D0E 60         RTS
0D0F 8C 08 7F   .OVF STY SCREEN
0D12 60         RTS
```

Example 4.3. Testing for overflow.

Try entering 127 and 1. Note the character displayed at the bottom of the listing is 'V', signifying overflow has occurred (the largest positive number in a byte is 127).

Now try entering 255 and 255 which results in an 'S', signifying that the sum is valid! This could seem incomprehensible until it is realised that 255 decimal is 11111111 in binary (FF hex) which, in two's complement form is −1. The result of adding −1 to −1 is −2, which is quite within the capability of ADC action. Finally, try entering 128. This will cause overflow and will output a 'V'. Mysterious perhaps, but 128 decimal is 80 hex and, in two's complement, is −128. Adding two of these is outside the capacity of a single byte register, hence the 'V' ouput. You are strongly advised to experiment with a wide range of input numbers to get two's complement firmly in your blood. It will be a great help when you reach a more advanced standard. Before leaving this example, note the SCREEN has been initialised to 32520 instead of our customary 32320. This is because the assembly listing is longer than in previous examples and the available clear space is lower down the screen.

Comparisons

Codes like BNE or BEQ are testing for the presence of *zero*. In fact they mean branch if not equal (or equal) to zero as the case may be. There will often be a requirement to test for the presence of a certain number other than zero. This can be achieved in either of two ways:

(a) By starting a register with the number, decrementing to zero and testing with BNE until zero is detected.
(b) Starting with a register empty and incrementing. After each increment, one of the *compare* instructions, followed by BNE can be used. This is a slightly longer method (one line more) but more flexible.

Table 6 defines the comparison codes.

Table 6. Comparison operations.

Mnemonic op-code	Action
CMP	Compare contents of the accumulator with the number defined by the operand
CPX	Compare contents of the X-register with the number defined by the operand
CPY	Compare contents of the Y-register with the number defined by the operand

The compare instructions do not alter the contents of the registers or the operand data. The comparison is done by performing a trial subtraction in a separate register so as not to degrade the active register's data. The direction of subtraction is always 'Register – Operand'. After the subtraction, the relevant bits in the PSR are updated as follows:

If operand data = register data, both the Z and C bits are set.
If operand data is *less* than register data, C is set and Z is reset.
If operand data is greater than register data, both C and Z are reset.
If operand data is less than or equal to register data, C is set.

It is important to realise that there is no point in using a *compare* instruction unless you follow it immediately by one of the *branch* tests. The *compare* instruction produces the PSR bits; the *branch* tests them. Example 4.4 is a simple example to get the feel of 'comparison' by incrementing the X-register until it equals the number entered in line 30.

The final content of X is first stored in &0DFF and later pulled back into BASIC by using the byte operator (?). Line 190, although BASIC, looks a little involved. The tilde (~) operator simply means 'print out in hex'; the '?' means 'the contents of' the hexadecimal address 0DFF. When the program is RUN, the number entered in decimal will match the hex number printed out, confirming that the comparison CPX and the following BNE have done their job correctly.

Example 4.5 illustrates various branch instructions as well as

```
10 REM *EXAMPLE 4.4 COMPARISON*
20 MODE 7:CLS
30 INPUT"Enter number for comparison "Compare
40 REM_____
50 FOR PASS=0 TO 3 STEP 3
60 P%=&0D00
70 [
80 OPT PASS
90        LDX #0
100.BACK INX
110        CPX #Compare
120        BNE BACK
130        STX &0DFF
140        RTS
150 ]
160 NEXT
170 REM_____
180 CALL &0D00
190 PRINT"X now contains the hex number ";~?&0DFF
>RUN
Enter number for comparison 32
0D00
0D00
0D00               OPT PASS
0D00 A2 00    LDX #0
0D02 E8       .BACK INX
0D03 E0 23    CPX #Compare
0D05 D0 FB    BNE BACK
0D07 8E FF 0D STX &0DFF
0D0A 60       RTS
X now contains the hex number 20
```

Example 4.4. Comparing numbers.

consolidating the information on the comparison technique. A fixed number is in the accumulator and the number entered (N) is compared, using CMP. Note the order in which the tests are made:

First test (BCC)   Is C clear? If yes, operand must be *greater* so branch to GREA which displays '>'.

Second test (BEQ)   Since C is set, we ask is Z set? If yes, operand must be *equal* so branch to EQUA which displays '='.

```
 10 REM *EXAMPLE 4.5 COMPARISON*
 20 MODE 7:CLS
 30 PRINT"Accumulator IS CONSTANT at 20 decimal"'
 40 INPUT"Enter operand number for comparison "N
 50 SCREEN=32680
 60 REM_____
 70 FOR PASS=0 TO 3 STEP 3
 80 P%=&0D00
 90 [
100 OPT PASS
110        LDA #20
120        CMP #N      \OPERAND IS N
130        BCC GREA    \C=0
140        BEQ EQUA    \C AND Z=1
150        LDX #60     \ASCII FOR <
160        STX SCREEN
170        RTS
180.GREA LDX #62       \ASCII FOR >
190        STX SCREEN
200        RTS
210.EQUA LDX #61       \ASCII FOR =
220        STX SCREEN
230        RTS
240 ]
250 NEXT
260 REM_____
270 CALL &0D00

>RUN
Accumulator IS CONSTANT at 20 decimal

Enter operand number for comparison 21
0D00
0D00
0D00            OPT PASS
0D00 A9 14      LDA #20
0D02 C9 15      CMP #N      \OPERAND IS N
0D04 90 08      BCC GREA    \C=0
0D06 F0 0C      BEQ EQUA    \C AND Z=1
0D08 A2 3C      LDX #60     \ASCII FOR <
0D0A 8E A8 7F   STX SCREEN
0D0D 60         RTS
0D0E A2 3E      .GREA LDX #62      \ASCII FOR >
0D10 8E A8 7F   STX SCREEN
0D13 60         RTS
0D14 A2 3D      .EQUA LDX #61      \ASCII FOR =
0D16 8E A8 7F   STX SCREEN
0D19 60         RTS
```

Example 4.5. Testing for greater than, less than or equal to.

Third 'test'   This is not necessary because at this point, it can be assumed that C is already set and Z must be reset. These are the conditions for operand *less* than, so the character '<' can be displayed.

The program exits (by RTS) at any one of the three positions, which indicates that the 'laws of structure' have been violated – modules should have one input and one output! It is not easy in machine code to obey such laws. 'Structure' is fundamentally a high-level language concept. It is unconcerned with execution speed but very much concerned with elegance and readability. Machine code is used primarily to save memory and to speed up execution. If too strong an attempt is made to twist machine code into structured form then the primary qualities may be sacrificed.

Flowcharts

Programs with plenty of branch actions can be very difficult to follow from an assembly listing and various diagramatic aids exist. The more traditional, but not necessarily the currently respected,

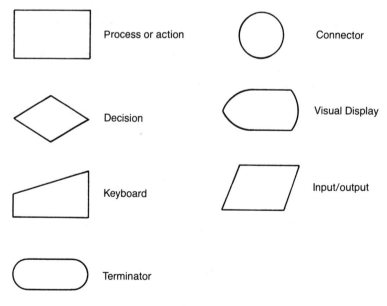

Fig. 4.2.   Standard flowchart symbols.

forms are the *flowchart* symbols shown in Figure 4.2. The outlines
are standardised but what is written inside them is the responsibility
of the programmer. The two fundamental outlines are the process
(rectangle) and the decision (diamond). Too much detail written in a
box can be counter-productive to the aim – to gain a broad outline of
the data flow. It is pointless enclosing actual mnemonic op-codes all

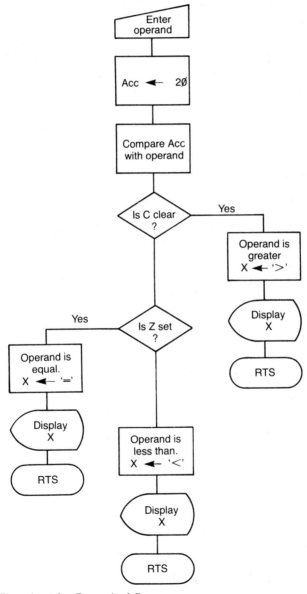

Fig. 4.3. Flowchart for Example 4.5.

over the place because the flowchart would then become a 'copy' of the listing rather than a supplementary aid to its understanding. To illustrate the use of a flowchart, examine Figure 4.3 which may help to explain the various branches of Example 4.5.

I have always had a suspicion that a flowchart is usually written *after* the program rather than before. It should, however, be used to pre-plan a program rather than be a device for 'post-explanation'.

The BIT test

The *compare* op-codes, CMP, CPX and CPY are used to investigate the whole of a byte. There are times, however, when certain bits in a byte have individual importance. For example, the bit pattern sent out to the user port is often used to switch, or receive yes/no signals from several unrelated sources. The pattern would therefore have no arithmetical significance and each bit would be unrelated to the others. The BIT test allows specific bits to be tested but, to obtain the full value of the code, requires familiarity with the class of instructions known as 'logical'. It is better not to deal with these at the moment. Fortunately, the BIT test can still be valuable without logic knowledge because it enables the state of bit-6 and bit-7 to be tested. (Bit-7 is the msb and bit-6 is the one next to it.)

Mnemonic op-code	Action
BIT	If bit-7 of the operand is 1, the N-bit in PSR is made 1
	If bit-6 of the operand is 1, then V-bit is made 1

Example:
BIT 32564: will examine the decimal address 32564 and update the PSR bits as described above.

It may be puzzling why bit-7 and bit-6 have been given VIP status over the other bits. Bit-7 is, of course, the sign-bit in two's complement but it is also an important link in *interrupt* handling. Bit-6 is also special in this way. It is not proposed to deal with interrupt facilities in this book although a pretty hefty dollop of theory is offered in the next one.

The BIT test, like the CMP test, must be followed by one of the branch instructions. Thus, if BIT is followed by BMI, a negative number can be detected in an operand. One important difference in the BIT test is that, unlike CMP, there is no need to bother the accumulator. There is no dummy subtraction although, when the extra logic functions are brought in, an AND operation does take place with the help of the accumulator.

Example 4.6 may help in understanding the BIT test, providing the program is understood! A number is entered (under BASIC) and is stored in 0DFF. This is done to emphasise that the BIT test can be conducted whilst the operand is still in memory. After the test (in line 120) a problem arises with regard to the display of the PSR. There is no instruction to 'Store SWR'. It is possible, however, to push it onto the stack with PHP and then pull it back into the safety of the accumulator and subsequently store.

The program should be run many times in order to consolidate previous work. The final hex figure result, F0 in the example run, should be scribbled out in binary before trying to relate it to the PSR contents. Thus, F0 is 1111 0000. Referring back to Figure 4.1, the bits in the PSR are then seen to be:

N=1   Indicating the operand has caused bit-7 to be set.
V=1   Indicating the operand has caused bit-6 to be set.

The remaining bits are incidental but, for the record, bit-5 is *always* 1. Bit-4, the B bit, is 1 because the program has stopped or Breaked. The number originally entered in the example was 255 decimal so we expect the Z bit to be 0 (because the number was not Zero). Finally, the C bit is 0 because this was cleared by CLC in line 100.

There remains the I bit, which is the Interrupt disable. *Interrupt* is treated in the next book *Get More From BBC Micro Machine Code* so, for the moment, note that it is 0, indicating it is *not* disabled.

The following results should be studied, to see if they make sense:

Enter 0   Result is 32 hex which in binary is 0011 0010.
Enter 1   Result is 30 hex which in binary is 0011 0000.
Enter 128   Result is B0 hex which in binary is 1011 0000.
Enter 193   Result is F0 hex which in binary is 1111 0000.

Unconditional jumps

There are times when it is required to branch, whatever the conditions. This would be called an *unconditional branch* and, if provided in the 6502, would have been given the mnemonic BRA. However, there is no BRA, although it is possible to simulate one by

```
 10 REM *EXAMPLE 4.6 BIT TEST*
 20 MODE 7:CLS
 30 INPUT"Enter a number "N
 40 PRINT"The hex equivalent is ";~N
 50 REM_____
 60 FOR PASS=0 TO 3 STEP 3
 70 P%=&0D00
 80 [
 90 OPT PASS
100     CLC
110     LDA #N      \Number to Acc
120     STA &0DFF  \Store it
130     BIT &0DFF
140     PHP         \PSR to stack
150     PLA         \Stack to Acc
160     STA &0DFE  \Store
170     RTS
180 ]
190 NEXT
200 REM_____
210 CALL &0D00
220 PRINT"Process Status Register cont
ains "~?&0DFE" HEX"
```

```
>RUN
Enter a number 255
The hex equivalent is FF
0D00
0D00
0D00              OPT PASS
0D00 18           CLC
0D01 A9 FF        LDA #N       \Number to Acc

0D03 8D FF 0D STA &0DFF \Store it
0D06 2C FF 0D BIT &0DFF
0D09 08           PHP          \PSR to stack
0D0A 68           PLA          \Stack to Acc
0D0B 8D FE 0D STA &0DFE \Store
0D0E 60           RTS
Process Status Register contains
  F0 HEX
```

Example 4.6. Using the BIT test.

using one of the conditional branch codes and *ensuring* the branch takes place by suitable trickery. There is one aspect of the branch codes, however, which can be disagreeable. Although not previously mentioned, there is a limit on the *range* of the operand in a branch instruction. In all cases so far, our examples have used symbolic *labels* for branch destinations but this facility is provided only by kind permission of the assembler. In pure machine code which, of course, the assembler has the job of producing, the operand is a hex number which must not exceed two hex digits. Destinations with a higher address are considered positive and those with a lower address, negative. Since the highest positive number in a byte is 7F hex (127 decimal) and the highest negative is 80 (−128 decimal) it follows that these are the limits of *relative* addressing. In plain English, the furthest forward we can branch is 127 bytes and the furthest backward is 128 bytes. If it is intended to branch outside these limits, a new type of 'branch' is needed. The 6502 calls them 'jumps' and they are given in Table 7.

Table 7.   Unconditional jumps.

Mnemonic op-code	Action
JMP	Jump to the destination as defined by the operand
JSR	Jump to the subroutine as defined by the operand

The assembler allows symbolic operands (labelled destinations as in branch codes). There is still a limit to the range but this is academic because it is possible to access any address over the 64K map with JMP or JSR. JMP in BASIC is the familiar (over-familiar?) GOTO and JSR is equivalent to GOSUB.

Subroutines

Previous treatment of JSR leads naturally to the subject of subroutines, with which users of BASIC will already be familiar. However, it is advisable at this stage to investigate certain features which we can afford to take for granted in BASIC but not in machine code. Although users of the BBC Micro will probably have little use for the 'old-fashioned' GOSUB in view of the more sophisticated PROCEDURE, it should be understood that it is still a disguised subroutine. A GOSUB goes to a line number, a PROCEDURE goes to an independently chosen *label* and also includes provision for parameter passing. Nevertheless, whether it is a PROCEDURE or a GOSUB, the concept of a 'return address' is inherent in both. As soon as we leave the present sequential line number (or sequential address in machine code) there must be stored a return destination and, in both cases, the *stack* is involved.

When, in machine code, the mnemonic JSR is used, the return address is automatically pushed onto the stack and the machine 'jumps' to the location where the subroutine is stored. When the subroutine has been executed, the machine pulls back from the stack

```
10 REM *EXAMPLE 4.7 SR DELAY*
20 MODE 7:CLS
30 REM_____
40 FOR PASS=0 TO 3 STEP 3
50 P%=&0DDD
60 [
70 OPT PASS
80.DELAY LDX #255
90.Outer LDY #255
100.Inner DEY
110       BNE Inner
120       DEX
130       BNE Outer
140       RTS
150 ]
160 NEXT
170 END


>RUN
0DDD
0DDD
0DDD                OPT PASS
0DDD A2 FF          .DELAY LDX #255
0DDF A0 FF          .Outer LDY #255
0DE1 88             .Inner DEY
0DE2 D0 FD          BNE Inner
0DE4 CA             DEX
0DE5 D0 F8          BNE Outer
0DE7 60             RTS
```

Example 4.7.   Double loop subroutine.

the return address and promptly shoves it into the program counter, ensuring that the original flow is resumed.

In all our examples so far, the machine code portion (between the square brackets) has ended with RTS, indicating they were all 'subroutines'. And yet, where was the JSR which called them? The explanation lies in the close linkage between BASIC and the assembler. It is probable that nearly all machine code 'programs' written by home enthusiasts will actually be subroutines. Instead of JSR, which is a legitimate 6502 op-code, the keyword CALL is used from BASIC to call a machine code subroutine. Our examples have used CALL &0DFF because the programs have been located at this address. However, if it is required to use another machine code subroutine somewhere *within* the machine code area, it is not

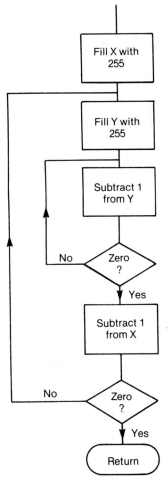

Fig. 4.4. Flowchart of the delay subroutine in Example 4.7.

permissible to use CALL because it is BASIC. We must use JSR.

Example 4.7 is a simple subroutine called 'DELAY' (note the label at line 80). If this is RUN, it will store itself in address &0DDD and be available for future use by any subsequent program which likes to use it. It will, of course, remain undisturbed by ESCAPE or BREAK. There are two loops, one inside the other. The inner loop revolves 256 times for each rev of the outer loop so the total revs $= 256^2 =$ 65,536. These 'useless' revs consume time but not much – a fraction of a second. It may be asked, why go to all this bother when the BASIC clock 'TIME' is available? In defence, the example was chosen simply to indicate how a subroutine can be stored and subsequently called up by name. The function of the actual subroutine is incidental when used for illustration. (See Figure 4.4 for flowchart.)

It can be called up by any other BASIC program, such as the following simple loop, providing we know the *address* where it was stored; the label DELAY will not work from BASIC unless it is previously assigned.

```
100 FOR A = 1 TO 10
110 CALL &0DDD
120 PRINT A
130 NEXT
```

The numbers 1 to 10 are printed with the delay interposed. To estimate the delay, run it again without line 110.

If the subroutine is to be called up by another machine code program, it will recognise the label DELAY. The calling line would be JSR DELAY. There are other ways of calling a subroutine from BASIC. The CALL keyword is equipped with powerful parameter-passing facilities and the alternative USR function is of great use. However, too much choise at one time can be confusing rather than helpful. It is more important to take these things slowly – it aids digestion.

Summary

- Unless otherwise directed, the individual op-codes (with their operands) are executed in strictly sequential address order.
- There are eight conditional-branches, BNE,BEQ,BPL,BMI,BCC, BCS,BVC and BVS.
- The operand of a branch instruction in pure machine code is a

two-hex-digit *relative* address, but the assembler allows an arbitrary label.

- All branch decisions are made according to the current state of the PSR bits.
- It is always the result of the *previous* instruction which determines whether or not the branch takes place.
- Destination labels must be preceded by a full stop.
- A branch can only be 127 bytes forward from the present address or 128 bytes backwards.
- Most programs written in assembly code require two passes before the equivalent machine code can be produced.
- The three comparison codes, CMP, CPX and CPY produce no action other than up-dating the PSR. They must be followed by one of the branch codes.
- Flowcharts may help in the pre-planning of a program. They are also of great help in explaining how it works.
- The BIT test, like the comparison codes, merely update the PSR. Bit-6 and bit-7 in the operand data determine the same bits in the PSR.
- The BIT test can be carried out directly on a memory addressed location without necessarily being involved with the accumulator.
- Unconditional jumps, JMP and JSR, can have destinations anywhere in the 64K memory area. Unlike the branch codes, they have no forward or backward limit.
- To use a machine code subroutine within a machine code program, JSR is used to call it up.
- The keyword CALL or USR is used to call a machine code subroutine from BASIC.

Chapter Five
Indexed Addressing and ROM Subroutines

Address modification

The best way to learn indexed addressing is by plunging straight in at the deep end with a program – so study Example 5.1 with great care.

```
  10 REM *EXAMPLE 5.1 INDEXED LOOP*
  20 MODE 7:CLS
  30 REM_____
  40 FOR PASS=0 TO 3 STEP 3
  50 P%=&0D00
  60 [
  70 OPT PASS
  80         LDX #0   \Initialise X
  90         LDA #36 \ASCII for $
 100.BACK    STA 32304,X
 110         INX
 120         CPX #240
 130         BNE BACK
 140         RTS
 150 ]
 160 NEXT
 170 CALL &0D00
 180 END

>RUN
0D00
0D00
0D00                OPT PASS
0D00 A2 00          LDX #0   \Initialise X
0D02 A9 24          LDA #36 \ASCII for $
0D04 9D 30 7E .BACK STA 32304,X
0D07 E8             INX
0D08 E0 F0          CPX #240
0D0A D0 F8          BNE BACK
0D0C 60             RTS
```

Example 5.1. Using indexed addressing.

The end result is 240 dollar signs printed on the lower half of the screen, achieved mainly by the 'magic' inherent in line 100. Clearly, the first mystery requiring explanation is the meaning of:

STA 32304,X

The STA part is obviously storing the accumulator in address 32304. This address is the leftmost character position about halfway down on the Mode 7 screen. So we can assume that the contents of the accumulator (ASCII for the dollar sign) will eventually appear in this position. But what is the significance of the comma followed by X?

X is, of course, the X-register but it is being used in its true capacity as an *index register* for the first time. In previous programs, the X-register has been employed on comparatively mundane duties. Here, it comes into its own as an address *modifier*. The rule is as follows:

To find the effective address of an indexed instruction, the operand address and the contents of X are first added together. The result is the effective address.

A few examples may help to clarify the above:

The operand is fixed at 32304. If X is 0, then the effective address is 32304 + 0 = 32304. Thus if X is zero, there is no address 'modification'. If X is 5, the effective address is 32304 + 5 = 32309. Finally, if X eventually 'grows' to 240, as it does in Example 5.1, the effective address is 32304 + 240 = 32544.

The essential quality of *indexed addressing* is the ability to make one instruction act on a variety of addresses, providing the index register is changed each time round a loop. Referring to Example 5.1 again, note that the index register is changed each time round the loop by INX. X is initialised to 0 in line 80 and increased by one each time round the loop. Before branching to BACK, the comparison code CPX checks to see if X has yet reached 240. When this value is finally reached, the loop exits. Because the address is increased each time round, the dollar sign is printed in the next screen positions. The flowchart in Figure 5.1 may help. Consider how cumbersome this program would have looked if indexed addressing was not available. It would have this appearance:

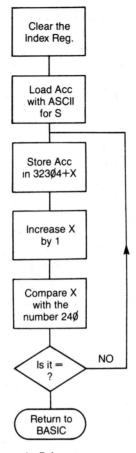

Fig. 5.1. Flowchart for Example 5.1.

STA 32304
STA 32305
STA 32306
ad nauseam until
STA 32544

Although the X-register has been used in the example, the Y-register could have been used because it is also capable of address modification.

Base, relative and effective address

Here are a few terms and their definitions, representing traditional jargon. They may be of some use, even if only to increase your image at the local pub:

The operand is the *base* address.
The contents of the index register is the *relative* address.
The sum of the two is the *effective* address.

Since the X- and Y-registers are only 8 bits wide, the maximum relative address range is 256 onwards from the base address. This is one of the more severe (and justifiable) criticisms of the 6502 microprocessor. It is customary to have a 16-bit index register available so as to cover the entire 64K address range. Disgressing for a moment into the realms of history, it is interesting to note that the Motorola 6800 microprocessor was the ancestor (if this is the right term) of the 6502. The 6800 was equipped with only one X register but it was 16 bits wide. So, apparently, the designers of the 6502, in their wisdom, decided it would be better to have two index registers of 8 bits each. However, the 6502 has a far more powerful addressing mode, known as *indirect*, which makes up for the 8-bit penalty. With indirect addressing, to be discussed in the second book, it is possible to cover the full memory map in a single loop.

Using OSRDCH

Previous examples have not been 'keyboard interractive'. In Example 5.2 we have cheated a little by using one of the machine code subroutines already in the ROM which provides the BASIC.

There are a number of beautiful subroutines in ROM and, providing we know the hex address where they are stored, they are free for the taking. They are given rather funny letter groups which, until you get used to them, seem, like gibberish. They all begin with 'OS', meaning Operating System and the remaining letters are alleged to have mnemonic value. The one used in Example 5.2 uses OSRDCH which means, 'Read Character from keyboard and send to accumulator'. It is surprising how difficult it can be to write a bug-proof subroutine to 'read a keyboard character' so we must be thankful that it is provided free. Apart from the difficulty of writing such a subroutine, there is another reason why the existing operating routines (which affect input/output) should be used. The reason is connected with the *Tube* protocol. All owners of the BBC Micro are potential owners of the 'second processor' which connects via the rather mysterious interface known as the *Tube*®. The software driving the tube is very touchy about 'unauthorised' direct interference with the input/output system but lives harmoniously

```
10 REM *EXAMPLE 5.2 KEYBOARD CONTROL*
20 MODE 7:CLS
30 REM_____
40 OSRDCH=&FFE0
50 FOR PASS=0 TO 3 STEP 3
60 P%=&0D00
70 [
80 OPT PASS
90.START LDX #0
100        JSR OSRDCH \KB to Acc
110.BACK  STA 32304,X
120        CMP #42     \Is it *?
130        BEQ FINI
140        INX
150        CPX #240
160        BNE BACK
170        JMP START
180.FINI  RTS
190 ]
200 NEXT
210 CALL &0D00
220 END
```

```
>RUN
0D00
0D00
0D00                OPT PASS
0D00 A2 00    .START LDX #0
0D02 20 E0 FF JSR OSRDCH \KB to Acc
0D05 9D 30 7E .BACK  STA 32304,X
0D08 C9 2A    CMP #42     \Is it *?
0D0A F0 08    BEQ FINI
0D0C E8       INX
0D0D E0 F0    CPX #240
0D0F D0 F4    BNE BACK
0D11 4C 00 0D JMP START
0D14 60       .FINI  RTS
```

Example 5.2. Using OSRDCH subroutine.

with the existing ROM subroutines. These have been written with
the Tube software in mind. In view of all this, it is not advisable to
write your own subroutines for keyboard action – even if you feel
quite capable of the task.

The listing in Example 5.2 should be examined together with the

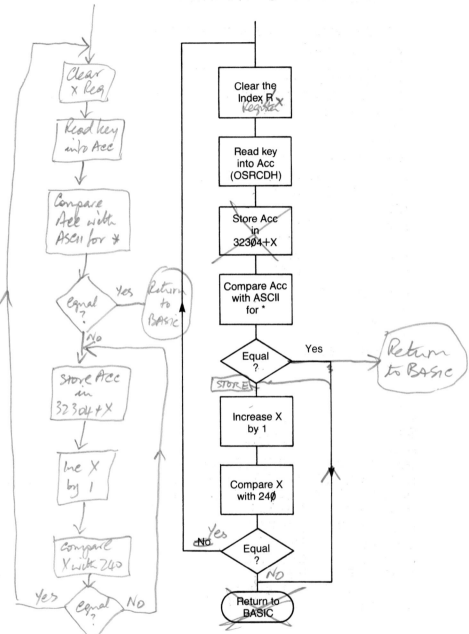

Fig. 5.2. Flowchart for Example 5.2.

flowchart of Figure 5.2. When the program is run, and any character key is pressed, a block of 240 similar characters appear on the screen. Pressing any other key changes the characters. The program remains in an endless loop, responding to the keyed character, until an '*' is entered. Only this character will cause the loop to exit.

The example is the first in the book to show up the high speed of machine code; the screen response appears virtually instantaneously. To compare the speed with the equivalent BASIC, enter the following few lines and note the sluggish response to a key change:

```
10 REPEAT
20 A$ = GET$
30 CLS
40 FOR A = 1 TO 240
50 PRINT A$;
60 NEXT
70 UNTIL A$ = "*"
80 END
```

Using OSWRCH

The object of Example 5.3 is similar to the previous example but, for the first time, we have left Mode 7 and its associated screen memory. Instead of using indexed addressing to store the accumulator on the screen, the subroutine OSWRCH is used. This resident subroutine is complementary to OSRDCH – instead of reading the keyboard into the accumulator, it outputs the accumulator to the screen. The flowchart is given in Figure 5.3.

OSWRCH stands for 'Write Character' which freely interpreted means 'send the contents of the acc to the screen'. The subroutine is written such that the printing position on the screen is under cursor control and it is automatically adjusted to whichever Mode is used. It is obviously far more flexible than our previous 'poking' to a memory location. Another advantage is the compatibility with the Tube, similar to OSRDCH. It may be strange to many readers why these resident ROM subroutines have been left till now. Why were they not brought into use in earlier examples? The answer lies in the title of the book. It would not be easy to 'discover' machine code if the groundwork was skipped in favour of the pre-written subroutines. A program, proudly presented as 'machine code' but which consisted of nothing more than a string of ROM subroutines would have little intrinsic substance to justify such pride. Carried to excess, the end result would develop into disguised BASIC. The language BASIC is, after all, a selection of ROM subroutines.

```
 10 REM *EXAMPLE 5.3 SCREEN CONTROL *
 20 MODE 4
 30 REM_____
 40 OSRDCH=&FFE0
 50 OSWRCH=&FFEE
 60 FOR PASS=0 TO 3 STEP 3
 70 P%=&0D00
 80[
 90 OPT PASS
100 .START LDX #0
110         JSR OSRDCH \KB to Acc
120.BACK    JSR OSWRCH \Acc to screen
130         CMP #42    \Is it *?
140         BEQ FINI
150         INX
160         CPX #240
170         BNE BACK
180         JMP START
190.FINI    RTS
200]
210 NEXT
220 CALL &0D00
230 END


>RUN
0D00
0D00
0D00            OPT PASS
0D00 A2 00     .START LDX #0
0D02 20 E0 FF  JSR OSRDCH \KB to Acc
0D05 20 EE FF  .BACK   JSR OSWRCH \Acc to
  screen
0D08 C9 2A      CMP #42    \Is it *?
0D0A F0 08      BEQ FINI
0D0C E8         INX
0D0D E0 F0      CPX #240
0D0F D0 F4      BNE BACK
0D11 4C 00 0D  JMP START
0D14 60         .FINI    RTS
```

Example 5.3. Illustrating machine code display speed.

Machine code can only be mastered by practice in arranging the op-codes to suit a particular objective. Your arrangement may be

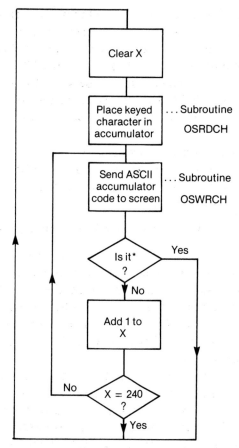

Fig. 5.3. Flowchart for screen control (Example 5.3).

inferior to the pre-written version in ROM (they are written by expert programmers with much experience) but they will have individuality and you will be learning all the time. Eventually you may even be able to improve on the expert versions.

However, you are strongly advised in the *User Guide* not to write your own subroutines which act *directly* on the input/output stream. This means the keyboard, the screen and the various filing systems so it is better to stick rigidly to this advice unless you have mastered the complete details of the operating system. This could take months or even years!

Relating OSWRCH to the VDU

The BBC Micro has been praised (and deservedly so) for its

graphics. The intricate hardware to handle the graphics is buried in a ULA chip on the board. With regard to the software, the rich selection of colour graphic operations are available as direct BASIC keywords or as one of the 'VDU' set (see page 378 of the *User Guide*). There is a very convenient 'bridge' between the VDU statement in BASIC and OSWRCH. Providing we master the bridging formula, a wide range of graphic effects can be controlled within machine code.

It should be appreciated from the start that OSWRCH (resident at the hex address &FFEE) is a most sophisticated subroutine, capable of far more than its title suggests. However, let's start by reaffirming its titled role:

OSWRCH   Write contents of Accumulator to Screen

Thus, whatever is in the accumulator at the time we write JSR OSWRCH, it is sent to the screen as a 'character'. If the accumulator happens to contain a number within the ASCII range for the standardised keyboard characters (ASCII codes 32 to 126 decimal) then this character is *displayed* on the screen at the cursor position. If we ensure that, say, 82 is planted in the accumulator, then JSR FFEE will display 'R'.

Codes between 0 and 31 are not strictly defined in ASCII and are known as *control* codes – they control or do things, other than displaying characters on the screen. They are best examined on page 378 of the *User Guide* which lists all the 32 control codes specific to the BBC Micro. Consider the example, VDU 7, which 'makes a short beep' on the internal speaker. The VDU keyword is, of course, BASIC so how do we make use of this in machine code? VDU in BASIC calls on subroutine OSWRCH anyway, so it is not surprising to learn that if we wish to employ it within a machine code program, JSR OSWRCH must be involved. But, since the same subroutine has to take care of all 32 control codes, it is left to the accumulator to inform which particular control code is to be activated. It is therefore up to us to ensure that it is popped in there before OSWRCH is called. So we need the following two lines to cause the speaker to beep once:

LDA #7
JSR OSWRCH

Perhaps it is as well to point out again that 'OSWRCH' is only recognised if it has been previously assigned to address &FFEE. If not, it must be written as JSR $FFEE.

However, this was one of the easy VDU examples because there was only *one* item of data required by OSWRCH, the number 7. Incidentally, numbers less than 9 are the same in decimal and hex so it is immaterial which form you use. The above LDA #7 could have been written as LDA #$7 but, clearly, the decimal form in this case would have been the easier of the two.

Many of the VDU forms are more complex and OSWRCH requires more 'information' before it can complete its allotted task. There will *always* be at least one data item, the control code, but the number of additional items, if any, can be as many as nine. (See page 378 again in the *User Guide* under the column heading 'Bytes extra'.)

For example, VDU 17 is used to define the text colour. Assuming that we are in Mode 1 and that we write VDU 17,2 the text will be in yellow. Here is a case where the OSWRCH routine requires two items of data, one for the code and one to inform which particular colour out of the four is available in Mode 1. Since all data sent to OSWRCH must arrive via the accumulator, then it follows that each item must be separately assigned. Thus, to cause text to be yellow, the machine code version of VDU 17,2 becomes:

```
LDA #17
JSR OSWRCH
LDA #2
JSR OSWRCH
```

The subroutine is designed such that once it receives its *first* data item (which is always the code) it 'knows' how many more deliveries to expect via the accumulator. There is a danger here. If you are not certain how many deliveries are required or perhaps miscount by one, the subroutine will scoop up the next byte (even if it was not intended to be part of the VDU command). This could have catastrophic results to your program, although it provides temporary 'excitement'. To guard against this, always look up the equivalent VDU statement in BASIC to ensure you know exactly how many bytes OSWRCH needs.

Semicolons and commas

This may seem a silly title but you can get into a lot of trouble when converting VDU forms to OSWRCH forms unless you distinguish semicolons from commas. Let's take one of the mixed forms, used to define a graphics window:

VDU 24,left;bottom;right;top;

VDU 24 is used to set a *graphics* window and in BASIC, a particular setting could be, say:

VDU 24,200;100;1000;500;

An obvious problem arises with the accumulator capacity. It is only one byte wide so the maximum number is 255 decimal. The problem is overcome by sending the numbers in two instalments according to the rule, 'low byte–high byte'. To work this out in machine code, it is first necessary to convert the numbers to hex. This can be done easily by direct commands to the machine using the 'tilde' (~). PRINT~1000 gives the hex equivalent as 3E8, which in two separate-byte form is 03 E8. But these must be entered low-byte *first* so, as far as the accumulator is concerned, we first send E8 and then 03. Even if the number is within the capacity of the accumulator, it is still necessary to send it in two-byte form. Thus the decimal number 200, when converted to hex, is only C8 and yet this must be thought of as 00 C8. The accumulator is therefore expecting C8 first and 00 next.

Returning now to the subject of semicolons and commas, the rule is:

If a semicolon follows the number, it must be two bytes.
If a comma follows a number, it is only one byte.

The above example VDU 24,200;100;1000;500; is the BASIC format but in machine code it will require a total of 9 bytes – one for the code 24 and two each for the other four numbers.

If you refer to page 378 of the *User Guide* which is the 'VDU code summary', the column headed 'Bytes extra' may now have more meaning. Looking up VDU 24, the number of 'extra' bytes is given as 8. This, of course, means extra to the VDU code byte (24), making a total of 9 bytes. The four decimal numbers are thus sent in hex form, in the following reverse-byte order:

200 = C8 00		100 = 64 00	
1000 = E8 03		500 = F4 01	

Example 5.4 sets a graphics window assuming the above parameters. When this is run, the lines 330 and 340 will prove the small graphics window has been set as programmed. The effect is a red rectangle, left superimposed over the assembly listing. It is worth checking with the graphics chart on page 495 of the *User Guide*.

It is quite clear from the example that using machine code just to

```
 10 REM *EXAMPLE 5.4 VDU 24*
 20 MODE 1
 30 REM_____
 40 OSWRCH=&FFEE
 50 REM *MACHINE CODE VERSION OF
 60 REM *VDU 24,200;100;1000;500;
 70 FOR PASS=0 TO 3 STEP 3
 80 P%=&0D00
 90[
100 OPT PASS
110 LDA #24       \CODE
120 JSR OSWRCH
130 LDA #&C8      \200
140 JSR OSWRCH
150 LDA #&00
160 JSR OSWRCH
170 LDA #&64      \100
180 JSR OSWRCH
190 LDA #&00
200 JSR OSWRCH
210 LDA #&E8      \1000
220 JSR OSWRCH
230 LDA #&03
240 JSR OSWRCH
250 LDA #&F4      \500
260 JSR OSWRCH
270 LDA #&01
280 JSR OSWRCH
290 RTS
300 ]
310 NEXT
320 CALL &0D00
330 GCOL 0,129
340 CLG
```

Example 5.4. Setting the graphics window.

set a graphics window is not exactly a simple or indeed a concise method. It is unlikely that it would ever be a worthwhile alternative to the relatively simple BASIC version. It would be better to nip back quickly into BASIC for such a task and then return to machine code again. This is the beauty of BBC assembly language, the ease with which you can enter and depart from machine code. However, the example was intended only as a guide to the entry of double-byte numbers and the significance of commas and semicolons when writing to OSWRCH. It would have been possible to save a few odds and ends in the coding. For example, the assembler is 'clever' enough to handle line 150, LDA #&00 as LDA #0 but, in the interests of uniformity and to keep faith with the previous text on double-byte numbers, two hex digits have been used throughout.

Using OSBYTE

BBC BASIC allows a certain amount of interference with the internal operating system, using the FX format. The letters 'FX' are phonetic shorthand for 'Effects' and page 418 of the *User Guide* lists them all. Unfortunately, they are a bit of a mixed bag as far as the species of ROM is concerned. The majority of owners who purchased their machines before the first month or so of 1983 were unlucky enough to have the first version of the operating system in a '0.1 ROM'. This version was a rather rushed job, 99% superb but cursed with a few niggling features which were left to be ironed out in later versions. The major fault was a certain unreliability during cassette tape loading, particularly with long data tapes. This was not serious for long because Acorn gave their blessing to a short machine code 'patch' which could be entered to circumvent the problem. Apart from this, the main defects were omissions, rather than errors, in software. The next ROM (or rather EPROM) to appear was entitled the 1.0 version which was intended, presumably, to replace the earlier 0.1 version. But it appears that even this new version was only given 'temporary' status giving way to the final definitive version which is the 1.2 ROM. Change and improvement is always exciting but is always at the expense of something or other. As far as we are concerned, the changes leaves the use of FX calls subject to certain provisos. Some work on system 0.1, others will not, so it is necessary to check the *User Guide* for guidance.

Before examining OSBYTE it is helpful to relate it to the FX format which, in the general case has three parameters:

*FX code, first parameter, second parameter

The *code* defines which particular effect is required and the parameters provide any additional information required by the function. Not all FX codes require both parameters; some require neither of them. FX is called from BASIC but, in machine code, the equivalent subroutine is names OSBYTE and is called with JSR &FFF4.

The name 'OSBYTE' provides a clue to the parameters required –

they are only one byte wide. This should be a relief; no worries about working out double bytes in reverse order. The accumulator and the two index registers must, in the general case, supply the parameters in the following order:

1. Accumulator supplies the code
2. X-register supplies the first parameter
3. Y-register supplies the second parameter

It is up to the machine code programmer to set the required values in these registers *before* using JSR &FFF4. If any of the parameters are not necessary for the particular code, the appropriate X or Y register is automatically set to 0. With some codes, the subroutine will supply 'answers' back again in the X or Y registers.

To illustrate the use of OSBYTE and the required register data, study the following:

(a) To flush printer output buffer use OSBYTE 21,3 the machine code would be:

    LDA #21
    LDX #3
    JSR &FFF4

(b) To disable all analogue/digital channels use OSBYTE 16,4 the machine code would be:

    LDA #16
    LDX #4
    JSR &FFF 4

(c) To read ADC channel into X and Y use OSBYTE 128,3 the machine code would be:

    LDA #128
    LDX #3
    JSR &FFF4

The parameter (3 in this example) is the channel number which is any one between 1 and 4 inclusive. On return from OSBYTE, the current AD conversion value is available in X and Y. Both registers must share the result because the maximum conversion number is outside the range of a single register. X contains the low-order byte and Y the high-order byte.

Note that the last example is one which uses the X-register to *supply* the necessary information before JSR &FFF4 is used but the contents after return is the *result* of OSBYTE action.

If OSBYTE 128 is called without any following parameters, it refers to the 'firing buttons' on the A/D device. The two least significant bits of X on return from OSBYTE will indicate which, if any, of the buttons have been pushed. Any other bits in X must be considered as dangerous garbage and must be 'masked out'. Masking out bits is carried out with logic operations (op-codes AND,ORA and EOR) which are discussed later. It would be unprofitable to give the full (formidable) list of all the OSBYTE calls in this book. To do so would be repeating good information already existing in the *User Guide*, pages 416 to 441.

Using OSWORD

Operating system subroutines which require, or deliver, more information than can be handled by using only the three registers are catered for by OSWORD. The term 'word' in traditional computing jargon was used to describe the maximum number of bits which could be passed to or from memory in one go. It was essentially a main-frame term because the 'word length' was seldom less than 32 bits and, in some of the larger giants, as many as 128 bits. The term 'byte' was then needed to refer to subdivision of the 'word' into manageable groups of 8 bits. So a computer with a word length of 32 bits would consist of four bytes. Because the BBC Micro can eventually be expanded to a second processor system and the *internal* architecture of the microprocessor used will be 32 bits, it was logical to call a collection of four bytes a 'word'. However, OSWORD calls are not limited to four bytes. In fact, the parameters required by, or delivered to, OSWORD are steered to a particular block in memory, the machine code programmer having the power to decide where the block should be. It is also the programmer's responsibility to ensure that any necessary data is sent to the parameter block before using OSWORD.

OSWORD is called from address &FFF1 and the address of the parameter block must be set into the X- and Y-registers before calling. The low-order byte must be in X and the high-order byte in Y.

The accumulator, as usual, must contain the code which distinguishes which of the OSWORD facilities is required. There are twelve accumulator codes given on page 458 of the *User Guide* within the range A=0 to A=B (in hex). They are a mixed bag, including setting or reading the time clock, the internal timers in the VIA, pixel colours and sound effects. It is understandable that such off-beat functions demand a lengthy setting up process before the final JSR &FFF1 can be employed.

Example:
Assume the time clock is to be read. The accumulator must be *set to 1* first, because this is the code for 'Read the elapsed-time clock'.

The clock information is five bytes long, so a decision must be made where these five bytes of memory can be spared. Let's squeeze them in at the bottom end of our usual safe area, &0DF0 to &0DF4. The low-order byte will be in &0DF0.
The procedure for calling OSWORD then becomes:

```
LDA #1          (Code for read clock)
STX #&F0        (Low byte of result address)
STY #&0D        (High byte of result address)
JSR &FFF1
```

Note that it is necessary only to inform OSWORD of the *starting* address of the five bytes – it 'knows' that five bytes will follow. The result is in hex of course, with the lowest-order byte in 0DF0. The prior setting up for *writing* into the clock (setting it to a new starting point) will be more involved than the above. It is necessary to set the X- and Y-registers to the starting address of the reserved five-byte area first then fill up the five locations with the new clock data.

Before worrying about this added complication, study Example 5.5 which reads the clock by using OSWORD and utilises the block of addresses as described above. The lines 170 to 190 prove that the clock is being read by the machine code. Four locations, starting at address &0DF0, are printed out as a single number by using the 'indirection' operator (!). The numbers at the bottom were the result of the GOTO endless loop at line 190. The print-out was stopped manually to save paper!

Storing at the top of BASIC

For consistency and to avoid cluttering the mind with too many alternatives, all our programs have been packed into the 'User Subroutine Area' which, in the Model B machine, is the 256 byte space at addresses &0D00 to 0DFF inclusive. It is better in the

```
  10 REM *EXAMPLE 5.5 OSWORD READ T*
  20 MODE 7:CLS
  30 REM_____
  40 OSWORD=&FFF1
  50 FOR PASS=0 TO 3 STEP 3
  60 P%=&0D00
  70 [
  80 OPT PASS
  90         LDA #1
 100         LDX #&F0
 110         LDY #&0D
 120         JSR OSWORD
 130         RTS
 140 ]
 150 NEXT
 160 REM_____
 170 CALL &0D00
 180 PRINT !&0DF0:REM 4-BYTE NUMBER
 190 GOTO170


>RUN
0D00
0D00
0D00                OPT PASS
0D00 A9 01          LDA #1
0D02 A2 F0          LDX #&F0
0D04 A0 0D          LDY #&0D
0D06 20 F1 FF       JSR OSWORD
0D09 60             RTS
```

Example 5.5. Using OSBYTE on four-byte numbers.

long run to use hex for machine addresses because it is the more concise notation and indeed, more logical. The third hex digit from the right in a four hex digit address is the 'page' number within the address map. Thus we can say that our programs have been allocated space on *page D*. However, if hex still remains an 'unnatural' counting system to you, then page D extends from 3328 to 3583 in decimal form. For those interested in the conversion method, the position of 'D' in the hex form is in the 16^2 weighting (256). Since D is thirteen in decimal, then 0D00 hex is $13 \times 256 = 3328$.

The advantage of storing in this area is purely *safety*. Any machine code loaded into this space is sacrosanct as far as the

ESCAPE and BREAK keys are concerned – it remains there until the machine is switched OFF or a 'hard-reset' is invoked.

There is one snag with page D however. It is not very big. It is surprising the power which 256 bytes of machine code can unleash but there will naturally be times when much more room is required. Providing the BASIC program interracting with the machine code is within reasonable bounds, a large space can be made available by using the DIM keyword of BASIC in a special form. The format is as follows:

DIM name N

As a specific example:

DIM PROG% 100

This means, 'reserve 100 bytes of memory above the BASIC program for a machine code program called BLOGS%'. (To be strictly accurate, this will reserve 101 bytes because the counting is from 0 to N rather than 1 to N – but why haggle over one silly byte?)

Note carefully that, unlike the normal DIM statement used to organise arrays in BASIC, there are *no brackets* used. The allocation of bytes is 'dynamic'. The actual address at which the

```
 10 REM *EXAMPLE 5.6 DIM P%*
 20 DIM PROG% 100
 30 REM_____
 40 P%=PROG%
 50 STORE%=P%+50
 60[
 70 LDA #20
 80 STA STORE%
 90 RTS
100 ]
110 CALL PROG%
120 PRINT ?STORE%
130 END


>RUN
0EC2
0EC2 A9 14    LDA #20
0EC4 8D F4 0E STA STORE%
0EC7 60       RTS
          20
```

Example 5.6. Locating machine code by using DIM.

machine code starts will depend on the length of the BASIC program. If we slip in extra BASIC lines, the entire machine code is 'dynamically' moved up. This seems a precarious situation but rest assured that everything remains under control – of the operating system, that is! Study the simple program shown in Example 5.6, particularly machine addresses allocated by the assembler.

Line 20 informs the system that a program called PROG% will inhabit a block of 100 bytes 'somewhere' in memory. The programmer leaves the responsibility of deciding *where* this block is located to the operating system. The starting address of PROG% is sent to the program counter (P%) in line 40.

Data, which requires storage space *within* the block, is named STORE% and, as line 50 shows, is 50 bytes ahead of the beginning. The exact number of bytes ahead is not too important providing it leaves sufficient room for the program. The number 50 was a conservative estimate, well on the safe side, chosen before the program was written. If you underestimate, data used by the program will be superimposed (overwritten) on the program bytes. If you are too generous, however, STORE% will stretch beyond the limits of PROG% and this is hazardous.

The machine code within the square brackets is quite trivial, merely storing the number 20 in STORE%.

The proof that 20 has been stored correctly is left to BASIC (line 120) which prints out the contents of STORE%.

Notice in the assembly listing the machine addresses which have been allocated by the operating system, 0EC2 to 0EC7 hex. To illustrate that the allocation is dynamic, write and additional line of BASIC, such as:

   25 REM THIS IS A TEST

and run the program again. The assembly addresses will all move up by the exact amount needed by the operating system to accommodate the extra line.

After a provisional run, it is easy to clean up the program. Thus it is obvious from the assembler listing that far too many bytes have been wasted by the provisional DIM allocation. It could fit comfortably, and with a few bytes to spare, in 20 DIM PROG% 20. A suitable data store would be STORE%=P%+15.

Mixing locations

Most programs require *data* of some sort or other. The program itself could be long but use only small amounts of data. Conversely, a program of a few lines could operate on vast amounts of data. To cater for all types, it is better to distribute the two sections. For example, to gain the added protection of the User Subroutine area in page D, it is often wise to place the machine code program there, but

```
 10 REM EXAMPLE 5.7 SORT DEMO
 20 DIM N% 200:REM PLACE FOR RANDOMS
 30 REM ___GENERATE 200 NUMBERS___
 40 FOR A=1 TO 200
 50 ?(N%+A)=RND(255)
 60 NEXT
 70 REM _____
 80 FOR PASS=0 TO 3 STEP 3
 90 P%=&0D00
100 [
110 OPT PASS
120.ITER  LDX #200  \LENGTH OF DATA
130       DEX       \LENGTH-1
140.BACK  LDA N%,X  \BRING NUMBER
150       CMP N%+1,X\NEXT NUMBER
160       BCS NOSWP
170       LDY#1     \FLAG
180       PHA       \SAVE ACC
190       LDA N%+1,X\SWOP PAIR
200       STA N%,X
210       PLA       \RETRIEVE ACC
220       STA N%+1,X
230.NOSWP DEX
240       BNE BACK  \NEXT PAIR
250       DEY
260       BEQ ITER  \IS FLAG 0?
270       RTS
280 ]
290 NEXT
300 CALL &0D00
310 REM ____PRINT OUT DATA___
320 FOR A=1 TO 200
330 PRINT ?(N%+A)
340 NEXT
```

Example 5.7. Ultra-fast machine code bubble sort.

if a large amount of data is required, it could be located by means of the DIM statement.

An obvious candidate for this kind of treatment would be a numerical sort program. See Example 5.7 which is using the DIM statement for storing 200 random numbers. The numbers are

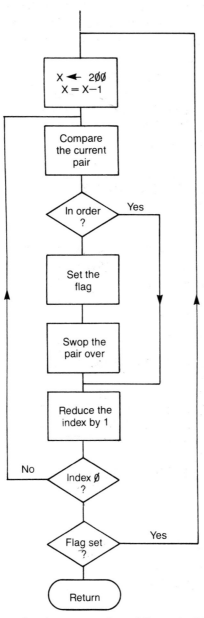

Fig. 5.4. Flowchart for the sort routine of Example 5.7.

generated by the BASIC lines 40 to 60 and include randoms between 1 and 255 (the largest pure binary number in a single byte).

The machine code program is stored in the User Subroutine space at &0D00 onwards. It is based on the well known 'bubble sort' routine in which each pair of numbers is tested for their correct order, lines 140 and 150. If a swop is found to be unnecessary, the program branches to NOSWP where the necessary preparation for the next pair is made. If a swop is required, it is carried out by lines 180 to 220 and a 'flag bit' is set in the Y-register. The procedure is repeated for as many times as the flag bit remains at 1. When it is found to be 0 it indicates that no swops were necessary.

The flowchart shown in Figure 5.4 will help to clarify the procedure.

When the program is RUN, the sorted numbers are printed out by the BASIC lines 320 to 340. Any slight delay experienced is due to the BASIC loops. The machine code sort, even although it is one of the most despised sort routines (in terms of execution time) is virtually 'instantaneous'.

Summary

- An indexed address has an effective value equal to the operand plus the current contents of the index register.
- Indexed addressing is identified by a comma after the operand, followed by either X or Y.
- Effective address = base address (the operand) + relative address.
- Subroutines resident in ROM can be used by writing JSR followed by the machine address of the subroutine.
- Resident subroutines having names beginning with OS (Operating System) are useful for communicating with the display screen.
- OSWRCH writes the ASCII character number in the accumulator to the screen.
- OSRDCH reads the character from the keyboard to the accumulator.
- Sending information direct to screen or other output devices is not recommended because it will interfere if the Tube is ever used.
- OSWRCH can be used to send control codes to the screen as well as ASCII characters.
- The VDU keywords, used in BASIC, can all be implemented in machine code using OSWRCH, providing the parameters are sequentially sent via the accumulator.

- When transposing VDU statements to the OSWRCH version, remember that a comma, terminating a parameter, signifies it is one byte but a semicolon signifies two bytes.
- Two byte operands in hex must be sent in the order low-byte then high-byte.
- THE group of statements in BASIC called FX can be converted to machine code by using OSBYTE.
- ALL OSBYTE calls require at least a following code, supplied by the accumulator. If more parameters are required, they are passed via X- and Y-registers.
- OSWORD is a powerful subroutine which requires too many parameters for handling by the three registers alone. The extra parameters must be placed in a memory block in the right order.
- The starting address of the OSWORD memory block must be sent via the X- and Y-registers. The low-byte of the address should be in X and the high-byte should be in Y.
- OSWORD sometimes places results back in the parameter block.
- Machine code programs can be stored outside the BASIC program space by using the DIM statement in a special way (without brackets round the parameter).
- Programs stored by the DIM method have not the protection afforded by the User Defined Subroutine area.
- The number of bytes reserved for the machine code program in a DIM statement is often a conservative guess in the first instance.

Chapter Six
Logical Instructions and BCD Format

Manipulating bits

Most of the op-codes in the 6502 repertoire act upon the complete byte. For example, the store and load operations STA and LDA, the arithmetic operations ADC and SBC are obvious examples of byte replacement and byte re-arrangement. There have been one or two exceptions, notably in the area of the program status register where each bit enjoyed a separate identity and consequently demanded special instructions to change the state. The carry flag has one of these special instructions to set it to 1 (SEC) and another to clear it to 0 (CLC). Another pair of instructions act on the *decimal* flag, SED and CLD. When this flag is set, the behaviour of the arithmetic unit is drastically altered. These flag bits are equivalent to a set of separate switches, not in the hardware sense of the term but programmable, *software* switches.

Apart from these specialised applications of the software switch, there is frequently a need to treat the contents of a register or memory location as a set of switches rather than a binary number, ASCII code etc. An obvious example of such a need is in the interface area to peripheral devices. We may want to connect wires to the user port in order to activate or detect signal changes in external gadgetry. Each separate gadget can be switched on or off by changing the particular bit in an output register which is dedicated to that gadget. It is understandable, therefore, that microprocessor designers always include a range of instructions which are capable of acting selectively on certain bits within a byte. For example, we may wish to change the state of bit 3 in address &0DFE without disturbing the remaining bits. It would be *possible* to achieve this by laboriously working out a number which, added to the contents of the address, would carry out the necessary selective change of bit 3. Mercifully, there are easier ways of achieving the task by using a set of op-codes which exist under the heading of *logical* instructions. Unfortunately, the word 'logic' has a variety of meanings in everyday language. To some, it is connected with clear thinking, to others it may conjure up visions of George Boole and his mind-bending algebra of classes.

As far as we are concerned, the 'logical' instructions are those having the following assembly mnemonic codes:

AND,ORA,EOR,ASL,LSR,ROL and ROR

All of them do queer things to the accumulator or, in some addressing modes, to the contents of a memory location.

Although they have some effect on the arithmetical value of a byte this must be considered entirely incidental. None of them are intentionally arithmetic in action although crafty programmers can sometimes trick them into producing valid arithmetical results. They merely change bits or push bit patterns along or remove certain bits altogether. Table 8 provides a formal definition of them:

Table 8.   Logical instructions.

Mnemonic op-code	Action
AND	Perform the logical AND operation between the pattern defined by the operand and the accumulator (the result being in the accumulator)
EOR	As above but perform the logical Exclusive Or
ORA	As above but perform the Logical Or
ASL	Arithmetic Shift Left the pattern defined by the operand
LSR	Logical Shift Right the pattern defined by the operand
ROL	Rotate Left the pattern defined by the operand
ROR	Rotate Right the pattern defined by the operand

The AND operation

The primary use of AND is to reset *selected* bits within the accumulator to 0, leaving the remaining bits undisturbed. To achieve this, a pattern of bits known as a *mask* is sent to the accumulator by means of the AND op-code. The problem is to work out first the particular pattern of bits which provide the correct mask.

It is easier to grasp the essentials by a preliminary example:

Problem: Ensure that the three right-hand bits in the accumulator are all at 0.

Solution: AND #&F8

Writing out F8 hex in binary, 1111 1000, may give some hint of the process. It would appear intuitively (to some!) that the mask must have '0's in those positions in the accumulator which are to be reset. The rule for the mask is indeed:

To clear bits to 0, place '0's in the mask to ensure corresponding bits are at 0.

Also place '1's in the mask to ensure that existing bits are unchanged.

Example:

Assume existing contents of accumulator were:	1011 1100
Mask bits:	1101 1111
After the AND mask the accumulator contents would be:	1001 1100

The mask has one '0' which has reset the corresponding bit in the accumulator, the other bits remaining undisturbed.

The ORA operation

The primary use of ORA is to set selected bits within the accumulator to 1, leaving the remaining bits undisturbed. Note this is the direct opposite to the AND operation.

The mask requirements are also the exact opposite to the AND case, the rule being:

To set bits to 1 place '1's in the mask to ensure the corresponding bits are at 1.

Also, place '0's in the mask to ensure existing bits are unchanged.

Example:

    Assume existing contents of accumulator were: 0010 0001

    Mask bits: 1000 1000

    After the ORA mask the accumulator contents

       would be: 1010 1001

The EOR operation

The primary use of EOR is to *change* selected bits within the accumulator, leaving the remaining bits undisturbed.

    The mask requirements are:

> To change bits, place '1's in the mask to ensure that the corresponding bits are changed.
> Also, place '0's in the mask to ensure existing bits are undisturbed.

Example:

    Assume existing contents of accumulator were: 0010 1101

    Mask bits: 1111 0001

    After the EOR mask the accumulator contents

       would be: 1101 1100

Boolean relations

There is a branch of mathematics known as Boolean Algebra which some readers may have studied, although those who have escaped seem to bear the loss with equanimity. The alternative definitions of the three logical operators are as follows:

    AND   If both bits are 1 then the result is 1

    ORA   If either or both bits are 1 then the result is 1

    EOR   If both bits are the same then the result is 0

All three operations exist in BASIC on the BBC machine but are used in what would appear to be, an entirely unrelated way to the descriptions given above. Take, for instance, the BASIC line:

    100 IF A = 4 AND B = 60 THEN etc.

This is using AND in the everyday usage of the term, having little resemblance to the 'bit-wise' usage. And yet, the two viewpoints are compatible (see page 205 of the *User Guide* for a well-written description of the relationship).

Practical uses

As previously described, a string of bits in a register is not necessarily interpreted by the programmer as a number or an ASCII character. It could represent information in coded form in which each bit indicates whether some condition is present or absent.

For example, it would be possible to store an employee's personal record in a bit pattern providing the code used was known and used consistently. Each bit would then represent 'yes' (if 1) or 'no' (if 0). There would clearly come a time when a particular bit required to be added or changed without affecting the other bits.

Even if the contents of a location did represent a simple number, it might be necessary to find out if, say, it were an odd or even number. We couldn't just ask it: 'Are you odd or even?'. However, if we cleared all bits to 0 except the lsb (the bit on the right) this bit would determine whether the number was odd or even.

Example: To find out if the contents of address &0DFF is an odd or even number:

```
LDA &0DFF
AND #&01
BNE 0DD
```

The number is loaded into the accumulator and ANDed with 01 hex. In binary, this is 0000 0001 which will clear all bits except the lsb. If the result is *not zero* (indicating that the accumulator must have had a 1 in the lsb position) the branch is activated.

When working out the correct mask, you should scribble out the binary bits required, then convert to hex. You can convert to decimal if you want but it is much harder!

Communicating with the outside world via the user port of the machine is another area in which the three logical instructions are valuable. These will be discussed under a separate heading. In the meantime, a few computer examples will help in getting the feel of the subject.

Example 6.1 is the 'find out how many odd numbers' problem, in the 200 random set. Every time an odd number is found, the Y-register is incremented.

```
10 REM EXAMPLE 6.1 'AND' DEMO
20 DIM N% 200:REM PLACE FOR RANDOMS
30 REM ___GENERATE 200 NUMBERS___
40 FOR A=1 TO 200
50 ?(N%+A)=RND(255)
60 NEXT
70 REM _____
80 FOR PASS=0 TO 3 STEP 3
90 P%=&0D00
100 [
110 OPT PASS
120        LDY #0      \CLEAR COUNT
130        LDX #200     \LENGTH OF DATA
140.BACK   LDA N%,X     \BRING NUMBER
150        AND #&01     \MASK
160        BEQ EVEN
170        INY          \ADD 1 TO COUNT
180.EVEN   DEX          \REDUCE INDEX
190        BNE BACK     \BRING NEXT NUMBER
200        STY &0DFF
210        RTS
220 ]
230 NEXT
240 CALL &0D00
250 REM ____PRINT OUT DATA___
260 PRINT"There were ";?&0DFF" odd out
of the 200"
```

Example 6.1. Distinguishing odd from even numbers.

Example 6.2 is another case of finding how many odd numbers but, to step up the heat a little, it also finds how many negative numbers there are and how many have a 1 in bit-2 position (remember that bit-2 is the *third* from the right in a byte). A flowchart is shown in Figure 6.1. To make it easier to check the validity of the results, the numbers loaded into the area above BASIC are the integers from 1 to 200. When this program is run, you should get the answers: 73 negative numbers, 100 odd numbers and 100 in which bit-2 was 1. If you don't see why this should be so, refer back to Chapter 2.

The user port

One of the numerous socket outlets of the BBC machine is called the

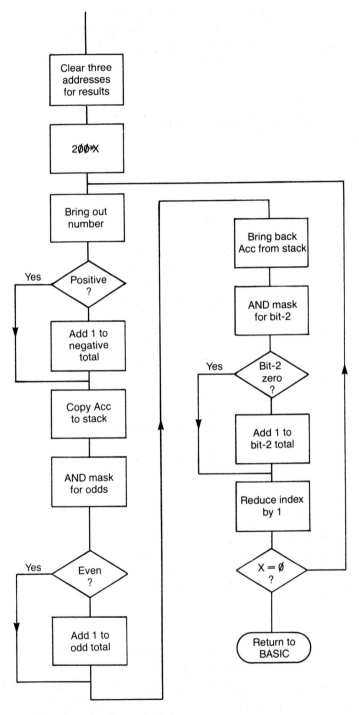

Fig. 6.1. Flowchart for Example 6.2.

```
10 REM EXAMPLE 6.2 COMPLEX'AND'
20 DIM N% 200:REM PLACE FOR RANDOMS
30 REM ___GENERATE INTEGERS 1 TO 200
40 FOR A=1 TO 200
50 ?(N%+A)=A
60 NEXT
70 REM _____
80 FOR PASS=0 TO 3 STEP 3
90 P%=&0D00
100 [
110 OPT PASS
120       LDY #0
130       STY &0DFC
140       STY &0DFD
150       STY &0DFE
160       LDX #200   \LENGTH OF DATA
170.BACK  LDA N%,X   \BRING NUMBER
180       BPL SKIP1
190       INC &0DFC  \UPDATE NEGS
200.SKIP1 PHA
210       AND #&01   \MASK
220       BEQ SKIP2
230       INC &0DFD  \UPDATE ODDS
240.SKIP2 PLA
250       AND #&04   \BIT 2 MASK
260       BEQ SKIP3
270       INC &0DFE  \UPDATE BIT_2
280.SKIP3 DEX
290       BNE BACK   \NEXT NUMBER
300       RTS
310 ]
320 NEXT
330 CALL &0D00
340 REM ____PRINT OUT DATA___
350 PRINT ?&0DFC" WERE NEGATIVE"
360 PRINT ?&0DFD" WERE ODD"
370 PRINT ?&0DFE" HAD BIT 2 AT 1"
```

Example 6.2. Searching a random list for odd and negative numbers.

user port. Like all the other channels for communicating with the outside world, it is 'memory-mapped', meaning that it occupies a block of machine addresses. The advantages of memory-mapped external devices has been exploited in most microprocessor designs. Because memory-mapping allows a peripheral port to be treated as a normal memory location, the entire instruction repertoire of the microprocessor is available for processing. It is not, however, proposed to delve too deeply into the user port. It is part of a very complex input/output chip known as the VIA (Versatile Interface Adaptor). The band of addresses from &FE00 to &FEFF have been given the strange but rather nice title of SHEILA. Within this band lives a variety of peripheral interface locations including not only the VIA but also analogue/digital converters, the ULA chips which handle the complex graphics, etc.

The VIA chip is a 6522 and occupies sixteen addresses, &FE60 to FE6F, but only two of these are of interest:

Address &FE60 (the user port data register)
Address &FE62 (the user port direction register)

The data register can behave as an output register or an input register but obviously it cannot be both at the same time. The ambiguity is resolved by the direction register which, once set up with the correct bit pattern, determines which bits in the data register are to be inputs or outputs.

Figure 6.2 illustrates the user port hardware lines to and from the outside world.

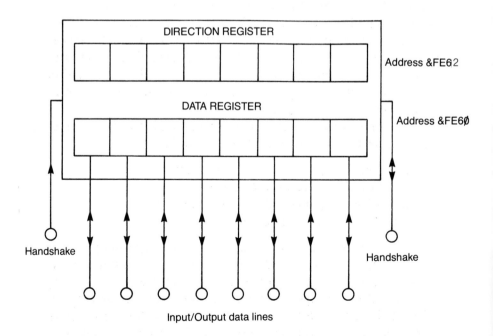

Fig. 6.2. Simplified diagram of the user port.

The rule for the direction register is:
Any 1's in the direction register define the corresponding lines in the data register as OUTPUTS.
Any 0's in the direction register define the corresponding lines in the data register as INPUTS.

Example: To make all eight lines in the data register behave as outputs:

    LDA #&FF   (put all 1's in the accumulator)
    STA &FE62   (store in direction register)

It is allowable to use a 'mix'. Some lines can be defined as outputs and some as inputs according to the whim of the programmer.

Example: To make bit-2 and bit-5 inputs and the remaining bits outputs:

    LDA #&DB   (1101 1011 in accumulator)
    STA &FE62   (store in direction register)

Setting the bits in the direction register is normally a one-off operation, serving to initialise the system at the head of the program. It is unlikely that the peripheral device, connected to the particular data line, is going to undergo a 'sex change' during the life of the program. Once an output, always an output!

It should not be thought that setting the direction register has any direct effect on the data register. The actual bits in the data register are defined by a separate address, &FE60. All the direction register does is to 'tell' the data lines whether they are to *deliver* information from the computer to the peripheral or to *receive* information from the peripheral to the computer.

To illustrate this, we shall first define all lines in the data register as outputs and then 'switch on' bits 2,3 and 7:

    LDA #&FF   (make all data lines outputs)
    STA &FF62   (direction register)
    LDA #&8C   (1000 1100 in accumulator)
    STA &FF60   (store in data register)

A word of warning is appropriate at this point regarding damage to the computer by haphazard connections to the user port. Unless you have some experience in soldering and have at least a smattering of theoretical knowledge of electronics, *don't* connect up external devices to the user port. If you want to practice with external lamps and switches connected to the port, either buy commerical plug-in 'boxes' or enlist the aid of a colleague who is an electronics buff.

Applying the logic op-codes to the user port

Although the data register behaves as a normal memory location, it is likely that each wire connected to the port is used as an entirely separate signal line. Suppose we want to ensure that the signal line connected to bit-2 is suddenly to be changed from 0 to 1 (switching 'something' *on*, perhaps). Clearly, if this line is independent from the others, it would be catastrophic if setting this bit to 1 altered any of the other lines. This is where the logic codes are so valuable because they are 'bit-wise' operations rather than byte-wise. You may remember from the definition of the ORA code that it is ideally suited for any task involving the setting of a 1 somewhere.

Example: First assume that all data lines are outputs. If we wish to ensure that bit-5 is in the 1 state without disturbing the remaining bits, we could proceed as follows:

```
LDA #&20    (0010 0000 mask for bit 5)
ORA &FF60   (Data register ORed into accumulator)
STA &FF60   (Store back in data register)
```

Suppose, instead, that we wished to *change* the state of bit-5 (instead of ensuring it was in the 1 state). The only difference in the above example would be to change ORA to EOR.

Finally, if we wished to ensure that bit-5 was in the 0 state, the appropriate logic code would be AND but remember the bit pattern must now be changed in the accumulator. The following example shows how this should be done:

```
LDA #&DF    (1101 1111 mask for bit-5)
AND &FF60
STA &FF60
```

Shift and rotate instructions

These four instructions, shown previously in Table 8, have one thing in common – they move the existing bit pattern. They behave as if there were a piston at one end, pushing the pattern along one way or the other. The difference between shift and rotate is whether or not bits are pushed out at one end and lost, or whether they are re-inserted at the other end in a closed loop fashion. In all cases, however, there is one mysterious extra bit involved, often referred to as the 'ninth bit'. This ninth bit is actually the carry (the C-bit), situated physically in the process status register of the micro-processor. However, from the programmer's viewpoint, it can be treated as a one-bit extension of the shifted or rotated byte. The following exaplanations should be read in conjunction with Figure 6.3.

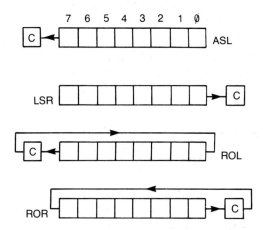

Fig. 6.3. Shift and rotate instructions.

Arithmetic shift left (ASL)

ASL has the effect of moving the bit pattern in the accumulator (or memory location) one place to the left.

Examples:

ASL A will shift the accumulator left.

ASL &0DFF will shift the contents of address &0DFF left.

Suppose the present contents of the accumulator are 0000 0111. After ASL A, the accumulator would now contain 0000 1110.

Note the arithmetical significance of this example. Before ASL, the accumulator contained 7 decimal. After ASL it contained 14 decimal, indicating that a shift left operation can be used to *double* a number. There is, however, an inherent danger that shifting left could, if the original number was large enough, cause a '1' at the left-hand end to drop out. This of course would result in an invalid multiplication by two. This is the advantage of the carry bit which is assumed to be a ninth bit extension. Instead of the accumulator bit at the end dropping on to the 'floor', it is caught by the carry bit. This means that, if we use ASL as a doubling up exercise, we should always use the BCS test to determine whether or not such a bit has been lost.

It is interesting to note, before leaving the subject, that a unique addressing mode called *accumulator addressing* is available on ASL and indeed the other similar operations LSR, ROR and ROL. These are the only four op-codes in the 6502 repertoire which have this addressing mode.

If we wish to use ASL on the accumulator then we must write ASL A. To write just ASL would provoke an error message from the assembler because it would be treated as an unrecognised code.

Logical shift right (LSR)
LSR has the effect of moving the bit pattern one place to the right.

Examples:
> LSR A will shift the bit pattern in the accumulator right.
> LSR &0DFF will shift the contents of address &0DFF to the right.
>
> Suppose the present accumulator contents are 0110 1000. After LSR A, the accumulator would then contain 0011 0100.

The arithmetical significance is the opposite to ASL because it *halves*, rather than doubles a number. As in ASL, there is a hidden danger if LSR is used for a divide by two exercise. If a '1' is spilled out of the register or location at the *right*-hand end, the arithmetical result is invalid. For example, if the original contents are 0000 0011 (decimal 3) and we shift right, the result would be 0000 0001 (decimal 1). Again, we can use the carry bit to test if this happens because it is effectively attached to the right-hand end of the register or location. Incidentally, why the shift right operation is called 'logical', rather than 'arithmetical', is due to the position of the carry in the scheme of things. It is natural for the carry to be at the *most* significant end, which indeed it is in the case of ASL. In LSR, the carry is at the *least* significant end which is 'illogical' from the arithmetic viewpoint – perhaps this is why the boffins call it logical! Yes, I find it confusing, too, but then I am not a boffin.

Rotate left (ROL)
ROL is still a shift left kind of operation but there is an end-around loop connection so that bits which are shifted beyond the carry position are reinserted at the least significant end. Unlike a normal shift, the bit *pattern* is never lost, it merely circulates. The carry bit is within the loop.

Example:

Assume existing contents of accumulator and
carry were: 1 0001 1100
After ROL A, the contents would be: 0 0011 1001

If, for example, you wanted to clear the left-hand nibble in a byte and replace it with the right-hand nibble the procedure could be a two-part one. First AND mask the left nibble to 0000 and then four ROL operations. This could have been achieved by four ASL operations but it is a question of individual taste. A better example for ROL action is the concept of a rotating '1', which is often useful in the area of user port devices.

Rotate right (ROR)

ROR is identical, except in direction, to ROL. Bits entering the carry bit at the right are re-inserted at the left.

Example:

Assume existing contents of accumulator and
carry were: 1 0001 1101
After ROR A, the contents would be: 1 1000 1110

Practical use of Rotate

Although ROL or ROR can be used for various trick effects, particularly by programmers with cunning minds, they are most useful in the input/output areas. Suppose the user port is connected to a set of eight separate devices and it is required to energise them one at a time in a sequential fashion from right to left (lsb first, msb last). This can be achieved by causing a '1' to rotate around the system. This assumes that a device is switched ON by a 1 and switched OFF by a 0. Strangely, depending on the logic circuitry which energises the device, the exact opposite may apply so it is worth digressing for a moment to examine the relationship between ON and OFF when applied to logic devices.

Devices which are switched ON by applying a '0' to the control input are said to be *active low* because, in a two-state system, the individual states are referred to as the HIGH state and the LOW state. A HIGH means a 'high' voltage although in practice this will be somewhere near 5 volts. A LOW, on the other hand, is a voltage near zero volts. Relating these relative values of voltage to our binary 1's and 0's, the convention is:

Binary 1 is the HIGH state.
Binary 0 is the LOW state.

Returning now to our original problem of switching devices sequentially (one at a time) it can now be seen that one of the following procedures must be chosen:

(a) If the devices are active low, we must cause a '0' to rotate round the data register. We start with every bit a 1.
(b) If the devices are active high, we must cause a '1' to rotate round the data register. We start with every bit a '0'.

Study the following, which illustrates the two methods of attack:

(a) Assuming active high devices:

```
        LDA #&00                (Place all 0's in output)
        STA  DATA REGISTER
        SEC                     (Place 1 in carry)
.BACK   ROL  DATA REGISTER
        BCC  BACK
```

The data register starts empty with all devices OFF but there is a 1 in the carry position. On the first rotate left, this carry bit is passed into the lsb position of the data register and the device connected to this position is energised. The C-bit is now clear.

Subsequent 'rotates' cause the solitary 1 to move progressively up the register towards the msb end, switching on each device momentarily on the way. The end of loop test causes a branch back while the C-bit remains 0. Finally, the bit from the msb is caught by the C-bit and the loop exits. Thus there is one complete cycle of device activity before the loop terminates.

(b) Assuming active low devices

```
        LDA   #&FF             (Place all '1's in output)
        STA   DATA REGISTER
        CLC                     (Place '0' in carry)
.BACK   ROL   DATA REGISTER
        BCS   BACK
```

This time, the data register starts 'full-up' but no active low device is working. The only '0' in the system is in the carry position. The first 'rotate' causes the '0' in the C-bit to pass into the register which switches the first device ON and a 1 at the far end is pushed into the carry. Thus the '0' travels along the register, switching each device on in turn until it finally enters the carry position. At this point, the loop exits because the test this time is Branch if Carry Set (instead of clear).

The coding shown is only to illustrate the procedure and is not suitable in the present form for entering into the machine. A complete program must, of course, prepare the data register for behaving as an output by initialising the direction register with all '1's. Also, the use of the symbolic operand (DATA REGISTER) would require prior assigning to the address &FE60. There is an additional factor, which has not been taken into consideration so far – speed. Suppose the devices in question were simple lamps and we expected that the previous program/s would enable us to see a light appearing to 'travel' along. The result would be disappointing because there would be nothing *visible* happening. The speed of the computer in switching the bank of lights sequentially is about four orders of magnitude faster than the human eye can perceive. Thus the burst cycle would be over before we could release the RETURN key. In all programs which energise external devices of 'brute force' dimensions like lamps, motors, robots or any form of logic-controlled machinery there may be some kind of 'time' interface to compensate for the differences in response time. The simple way to slow down the computer is by means of a delay loop, which could be spliced straight into the program or, alternatively, called as a subroutine.

Problems with the C-bit

A common bug, often difficult to find in assembly coding, is to forget that the C-bit (and indeed most other bits in the PSR) is automatically updated after most of the instruction codes. This can cause problems when testing the result of the C-bit because you could be testing it in the wrong place. For example, in the previous two examples of ROL, it may be thought that a delay subroutine could be inserted to slow the process down. Unfortunately, the state of the C-bit could very well have been altered by the subroutine causing the BCS or BCC test at the bottom to be based on incorrect information. This could very well cause an infinite-loop situation. It is easy t save the C-bit at its current value by pushing the PSR on the stack with PHP and retrieving it with PLP.

Examples to illustrate logic codes

Example 6.3 is a simple exercise in the shift left operation. Any number, subject to the limited capacity of a single-byte result, entered at line 30 will be printed out at line 120. The machine code is only three

```
10 REM EXAMPLE 6.3 ASL
20 CLS
30 INPUT"Enter a number "N%
40 ?&0DFF=N%
50 P%=&0D00
60 [
70          LDA &0DFF
80          ASL &0DFF
90          RTS
100 ]
110 CALL &0D00
120 PRINT"After ASL,your number is now
";?&0DFF
```

```
>RUN
Enter a number 33
0D00
0D00 AD FF 0D LDA &0DFF
0D03 0E FF 0D ASL &0DFF
0D06 60        RTS
After ASL,your number is now 66
```

Example 6.3. Use of Shift Left.

lines and because there are no branch forward operations, it is not necessary to pass twice through the assembler. The program should be tried out with various input numbers. If we assume the byte is unsigned integer, the largest number which gives a valid result will be 127 as input; the result being 254. However, if you try inputting 128, the result is 0. This is understandable if the bit pattern for 128 is written out as:

1000 0000   (128 in unsigned integer form)

After ASL, the msb is shifted into the C-bit position, leaving 0000 0000 in the location.

Example 6.4 is similar in structure but allows practice with the effects of ROL. The carry is set in line 70 in order to observe its influence on the result. During the example run, 8 was entered and, if it weren't for the carry, the effect of ROL would be to double it to 16. But the answer given by line 130 is 17 due to the carry circulating into the lsb position. You should try several different inputs to prove that, subject to the limitations of a single byte result, the program is producing $2N+1$.

Example 6.5 deals with ROR. Again, the carry is set in order to see

```
 10 REM EXAMPLE 6.4 ROL
 20 CLS
 30 INPUT"Enter a number "N%
 40 ?&0DFF=N%
 50 P%=&0D00
 60 [
 70         SEC
 80         LDA &0DFF
 90         ROL &0DFF
100         RTS
110 ]
120 CALL &0D00
130 PRINT"After ROL,your number is now
";?&0DFF

>RUN
Enter a number 8
0D00
0D00 38        SEC
0D01 AD FF 0D  LDA &0DFF
0D04 2E FF 0D  ROL &0DFF
0D07 60        RTS
After ROL,your number is now 17
```

Example 6.4. Use of Rotate Left.

its effect on the result. After ROR, the carry is pushed into the msb
position which is worth 128 in unsigned binary integer format. So, if
0 is entered, the result is 128. The example run shows that 5 was
entered, producing the result of 130 so we had better find out if this is
reasonable:

	carry bit		
Before ROR	1	0000 0101	(5)
After ROR	1	1000 0010	(130)

Note that the carry starts at 1 but, because the lsb was rotated into
the carry position, it is still at 1 after ROR.

The exclusive-or operation (EOR) can be used to produce the
logical complement of a byte:

Number	0110 1101	
Logical complement	1001 0010	(all bits reversed state)

This can be achieved by 'exclusive-oring' with all the 1's because you
will remember from previous work that any 1 in the EOR mask
pattern will reverse the corresponding bit of the number. However,
if an extra 1 is added afterwards, the result is the two's complement.

```
10 REM EXAMPLE 6.5 ROR
20 CLS
30 INPUT"Enter a number "N%
40 ?&0DFF=N%
50 P%=&0D00
60 [
70          SEC
80          LDA &0DFF
90          ROR &0DFF
100         RTS
110 ]
120 CALL &0D00
130 PRINT"After ROR,your number is now
";?&0DFF

>RUN
Enter a number 5
0D00
0D00 38          SEC
0D01 AD FF 0D LDA &0DFF
0D04 6E FF 0D ROR &0DFF
0D07 60          RTS
After ROR,your number is now 130
```

Example 6.5.   Use of Rotate Right.

Example 6.6 shows the effect of EOR #&FF on any number entered. The number 33 apparently turns into 222 which we can check as follows:

Number	0010 0001	(33)
FF mask	1111 1111	(FF hex)
Result	1101 1110	(DE hex=222 decimal)

It may be of interest to those who found Chapter 2 stimulating, to use this example to prove the two's complement version.

The result above is the logical or one's complement and by adding 1 the two's complement is obtained as follows:

	1101 1110	
add	1	
result	1101 1111	(DF hex)

Now this is a *negative* number if we consider it as a two's complement number rather than an unsigned integer and is representing -33 decimal. From this, it appears that if it is required to change N into $-$N, or *vice versa*, the coding lines would be:

LDA Number
EOR #&FF
ADC #1

```
  10 REM EXAMPLE 6.6 EOR
  20 CLS
  30 INPUT"Enter a number "N%
  60 ?&0DFF=N%
  70 P%=&0D00
  80 [
  90          LDA &0DFF
 100          EOR #&FF
 110          STA &0DFF
 120          RTS
 130 ]
 140 CALL &0D00
 150 PRINT"After EOR #FF,your number is
now ";?&0DFF
```

```
>RUN
Enter a number 33
0D00
0D00 AD FF 0D LDA &0DFF
0D03 49 FF    EOR #&FF
0D05 8D FF 0D STA &0DFF
0D08 60       RTS
After EOR #FF,your number is now 222
```

Example 6.6.   Use of Exclusive Or.

It is well to emphasise here that a number in any register or memory
location has the significance which the programmer attributes to it.
If the programmer wants it to be considered as a two's complement
number then the V-bit (overflow) in the PSR is meaningful. If it is to
be considered an unsigned binary integer, the PSR can be ignored.
Referring back to our example, whether we consider the 'answer' is
222 decimal or −33 decimal is entirely up to us!

Binary Coded Decimal (BCD)

There is still another way of representing numbers which, on
occasions, may be useful. It is called BCD for short and relies on a
sharp division of a byte into two four-bit nibbles.

Consider the following pattern:

1001 0111

In unsigned binary this means 151 decimal. In two's complement it means −107 decimal, but in BCD it means 97 decimal. The nibbles are independent of each other and are read as separate four-bit patterns; the high-order nibble is 9 and the low-order 7. The decimal digits 0 to 9 are written as simple binary 0000 to 1001. The six combinations 1010 to 1111 are *illegal* in BCD.

Troubles arise because of these illegalities if we try to add some numbers in BCD format. Some examples will show up the problem:

(a) Add 5 to 23   0000 0101   (5)
                   0010 0011   (23)
                   0010 1000   (28)

This result is correct and legal in BCD.

(b) Add 8 to 23   0000 1000   (8)
                   0010 0011   (23)
                   0010 1011   Illegal result

The lower order nibble is an illegal combination in BCD. However, a strange but relatively simple dodge can be used to legalise the result:

If the result contains illegal nibbles, add six.

To test this, refer back to the previous result:

Illegal result   0010 1011
Add 6   0000 0110
Result   0011 0001   Legal BCD for 31

So the procedure for adding BCD numbers would appear to be:

Test if either nibble of the result is illegal.
If so, add a further six.

This works because there are six illegal patterns after 1001. This is clearly a tiresome procedure but the 6502 micro has a powerful and rather unusual op-code called SED which handles all this automatically. SED means S̲et D̲ecimal Mode and causes a 1 to be set in the D-bit position in the PSR. Once this is set, the micro will assume that the arithmetic codes ADC and SBC are intended to operate with numbers in BCD format, making the necessary adjustments to avoid illegal results.

Once the D-bit is set, it will remain set until cancelled with CLD which means Clear Decimal mode. It is important to clear the decimal mode before you start on another program or you will get very strange results. Example 6.7 is a simple exercise to illustrate BCD addition. There are several pitfalls in using BCD which, unless you study the example closely, might cause trouble if you write your own programs. In the first place, it is important to realise that illegal codes *entered* are not automatically corrected by the SED action. All SED does is to correctly adjust the *results* of an addition to BCD – it will not correct illegals before ADC operates. Thus, when you enter the numbers, they must be single digits in the range 0 to 9. The program is sprinkled with remarks but the flowchart of Figure 6.4 should help in following the coding.

```
10 REM EXAMPLE 6.7 ADDING IN BCD
15 REM *ONLY SINGLE DIGIT NUMBERS*
20 INPUT"Enter first number "N1%
30 INPUT"Enter second number "N2%
40 INPUT"Enter third number "N3%
50 ?&0DF1=N1%
60 ?&0DF2=N2%
70 ?&0DF3=N3%
80 P%=&0D00
90 [
100         CLC
110         SED       \Set BCD mode
120         LDA #0
130         ADC &0DF1\add the numbers
140         ADC &0DF2
150         ADC &0DF3
160         PHA       \save Acc
170         AND #&0F \clear high nibble
180         STA &0DF4\low digit result
190         PLA       \get Acc back
200         LSR A
210         LSR A     \shift high nibble
220         LSR A
230         LSR A
240         STA &0DF5\high digit result
250         RTS
260 ]
270 CALL &0D00
280 PRINT"BCD sum is "?&0DF5;?&0DF4
```

```
>RUN
Enter first number 9
Enter second number 8
Enter third number 7
0D00
0D00 18         CLC
0D01 F8         SED        \Set BCD mode
0D02 A9 00      LDA #0
0D04 6D F1 0D   ADC &0DF1\add the numbers
0D07 6D F2 0D   ADC &0DF2
0D0A 6D F3 0D   ADC &0DF3
0D0D 48         PHA        \save Acc
0D0E 29 0F      AND #&0F \clear high nibble
0D10 8D F4 0D   STA &0DF4\low digit result
0D13 68         PLA        \get Acc back
0D14 4A         LSR A
0D15 4A         LSR A      \shift high nibble
0D16 4A         LSR A
0D17 4A         LSR A
0D18 8D F5 0D   STA &0DF5\high digit result
0D1B 60         RTS
BCD sum is            24
```

Example 6.7. Adding in BCD format.

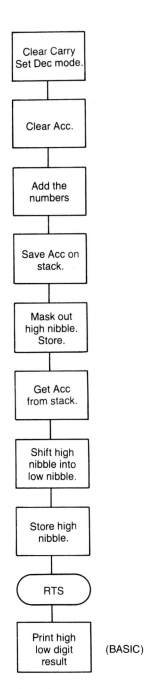

Fig. 6.4. Flowchart for Example 6.7.

Summary

- *Logical* instructions are used for bit rather than byte processing. They have op-codes AND,EOR,ORA,ASL,LSR,ROL,ROR.
- AND is used to clear bits to '0', ORA to set bits to '1' and EOR is used to change bits.
- The user port is positioned within a band of addresses known as SHEILA.
- The data register communicates with the outside world via 8 data lines and has the address &FE60. The direction register has the address &FE62 and is used to define which data lines are input and which output.
- Shift and rotate instructions are used to shuffle bits along the register or memory location, the C-bit acting as the ninth bit.
- To change the state of all bits, use EOR #&FF.
- BCD format treats each nibble separately; the highest decimal value allowed in each nibble is 9. The highest number in a byte is therefore 99 decimal.
- To cause the arithmetic unit to add or subtract in BCD, the D-bit in the PSR must be set by using SED.
- SED will only initiate correct BCD addition and subtraction if the operands contain no illegal patterns (above 1001).

Chapter Seven
Programming Guidelines

Mental attitude

Programming in BASIC is often a relaxing pastime. So much power appears available with such little effort because each statement triggers off a large number of hidden machine code instructions. It is rather like building a house from pre-fabricated walls and roof. The advantage of pre-fabrication is the relative ease and simplicity of erection; the disadvantage is the limitation imposed on the design.

Machine code, even with the aid of the assembler, is a slow painstaking operation due to the building-brick level of each instruction. Each line of assembly code produces only one line of machine code but the program can be structured with freedom and individuality apart from the occasional employment of OSWRCH, OSRDCH, etc. However, it is essential to cultivate the right mental attitude toward machine code programming. Until confidence is gained, which will take some time, the most formidable enemy is frustration. When you write a program in BASIC it *may* not work first time; if you write it in machine code it almost certainly will *not* work first time ... or the second or indeed the nth time in many cases. You are fighting the machine with its own weapons which are little more than flint axes and cudgels! The examples in this book, simple as they are, were no exception. In fact, only two of them behaved themselves first go but I have survived years of frustration. I seem to have reached the stage of feeling slightly disappointed if the first run is errorless! The great thing to remember is that grappling with the machine is essentially a learning process. Every time you clear a bug you have learned just a little more about the workings of the microprocessor which, after all, is the central processor of the computer.

De-bugging orgies

Fault symptoms are conveniently classified into the following neat categories:

(a) Nothing happens at all.
(b) Something is happening but completely different to what was intended.
(c) The program *nearly* works as intended.

Category (a), in which nothing happens at all, is often the easiest of the error situations. That is to say, the bug or bugs which cause it are often trivial and easily spotted. The following are some of the more likely causes:

- Forgetting to set P% before entering the assembly bracket area.
- Forgetting to CALL up the machine code.
- Forgetting RTS at the end.
- If the program was located by using DIM, it is possible that you have underestimated the number of bytes used.
- CALL with an incorrect address.
- Using one pass through the assembler instead of two.

Category (b) is also fairly easy to correct, perhaps due to:

- Use of STA with a wrong address causing a crash into an operating system area.
- The address could be correct as far as the digits go but perhaps '&' has been missed out, or inserted in error.
- Using the wrong branch code, say BNE instead of BEQ or BPL instead of BMI.
- Branch label in the wrong place.
- Using one of the registers without saving the original contents before use.
- Using the stack in the incorrect order – it should be last-in first-out.

Category (c) is often the most frustrating of all the error conditions, making it difficult to think up reasonable causes. However, try:

- Carry bit not cleared before addition or not set before subtraction.
- One out in a loop count – for example, forgetting that zero to four is in reality five counts not four.
- Mixing up immediate addressing with absolute addressing.
- Assuming a register is zero when in fact it starts with garbage in it.

- Mixing up DEX with DEY in a loop. This one is quite common.
- Forgetting the $+127$ and -128 limits of two's complement.
- Forgetting the 255 limit on unsigned integers.
- Failing to realise that an overflow condition is not an error as far as the microprocessor is concerned. It is up to you to test the V bit with BVS or BVC.
- Forgetting to clear decimal mode flag with CLD after use. The subroutines OSWRCH, OSWORD, etc. will not operate while the D bit remains set.

The assembler error messages will help, of course, but not to the same extent as we may be used to under the BASIC interpreter. It may be that the program is failing because of a bug in one tiny segment. It is often possible to nail down the offending line or lines by short-circuiting the suspect segment with a temporary JMP to the next segment. The program obviously won't be fully operational but, allowing for the inactive lines, it may be possible to locate the troublesome area.

It is quite common to misjudge the dividing line between the program lines and the data storage locations. Programs use data so it is natural that data is stored somewhere. If the storage locations have been haphazardly addressed, it is possible for the data to be deposited *within* the program area instead of outside it. The program is then corrupted by its own data. Wherever possible, data should be placed at the *end* of the program. You can get into a frightful mess if data and program lines are intermingled.

Although the above suggestions may be helpful, by far the most likely faults in the early stages are the result of careless input, particularly mistakes in absolute machine addresses. There will be a tendency to stick to decimal addresses because of familiarity, but effort should be made to stifle this inclination. After all, hex code is as natural to machine code addressing as decimal is to counting and arithmetic. If you use decimal numbers for addressing, you are increasing the chance of error due to the conversion process. All the operating system subroutines in the *User Guide* are addressed in hex and it is pointless converting these to decimal.

Allocating resources

Is there any point in writing a complete program in machine code? I think the answer to this depends to some extent on your temperament. It is certainly satisfying to the ego if a lengthy and complex program is written entirely in machine code. There is satisfaction in overcoming enormous odds – the Everest complex is present in most of us. However, overcoming difficulties just for the sake of overcoming them may be a desirable trait but seldom justifiable in terms of energy conservation. To restrict yourself to machine code will certainly demand a deal of mental energy, much of it expended in re-inventing the wheel.

The BBC Micro, perhaps more than any other machine available in its price bracket, appears to be designed deliberately to encourage a healthy mix between BASIC and machine code. Because of this, it is wise to optimise the resources available. There are several recognisable software tools in the machine. There is the standard BASIC language with its fairly advanced vocabulary, the set of powerful VDU statements, the operating system *FX statements, the machine code subroutines such as OSWRCH,OSRDCH, OSBYTE,OSWORD, etc. and the standard 6502 machine code repertoire. It seems to me to be quite pointless to use machine code in situations where BASIC lines can perform the particular sub-task without observable speed penalties. It is equally pointless to write your own machine code for tasks which are already catered for by the built-in machine code subroutines. Unless you are very experienced (in which case this book is not for you) you would be hard pressed to improve on OSWRCH or the other subroutines available.

Because the BBC system is so flexible it is easy to stick to BASIC but, wherever it is found wanting, leave it temporarily to activate a machine code splice and return again. In fact, it is not a bad idea to write the complete program in BASIC first and get it working. After this, it can be carefully scrutinised for time bottlenecks and the offending area earmarked for subsequent conversion to machine code. Apart from speed penalties, it may sometimes be more economical to use BASIC as far as memory economy is concerned. For example, I see little point in using machine code to output messages on the screen. The actual ASCII codes can, of course, be placed into chosen absolute addresses but the procedure to put them there might just as well be achieved with BASIC. To use the 'right tools for the job' is as true in software engineering as in nut and bolt engineering. Machine code can certainly give you enormous speed and power if it is used correctly and in its proper place.

BASIC structures and the machine code equivalents

Because BASIC is so well known, particularly amongst home enthusiasts, it is a good plan to be able to reproduce in machine code some of the familiar statements. This may be putting the cart before the horse but at least you will be treading on familiar ground. Some may argue that such a procedure is arguing in a circle. Why try to imitate BASIC with machine code? If BASIC is so slow, what is the point of writing machine code equivalents – won't they be equally slow? Such arguments, however, are based on a mistaken idea as to the prime cause of BASIC's slow speed reputation. All BASIC statements are translated to machine code but, due to the interpreter action, they must be translated each time they are run. If, however, they are simulated by our own machine code subroutines, they are in a direct form for immediate running. Once they have been assembled they are ready for use.

The following examples may be found useful for those who are familiar with BASIC since they are reasonable equivalents in machine code to the BASIC statements. The line numbers given are purely arbitrary, as are the labels and variable names. They are not complete programs and obviously cannot be run as they stand. They are, however, simple frameworks upon which useful programs can be designed. Be careful with the size of numbers because of the limitation on single byte working.

Assigning a constant to a variable:

BASIC example:	Machine code equivalent:
10 Speed = 30	10 LDA #30
	20 STA Speed

Assigning variables:

BASIC example:	Machine code equivalent:
10 S = B	10 LDA B
	20 STA S

Addition of a constant:

BASIC example:	Machine code equivalent:
10 S = S + 4	10 CLC
	20 LDA S
	30 ADC #4
	40 STA S

Subtraction of a constant:

BASIC example:	Machine code equivalent:
10 S = S − 25	10 SEC
	20 LDA S
	30 SBC #25
	40 STA S

Mixed addition and subtraction:

BASIC example:	Machine code equivalent:
10 S = S + V − 3	10 LDA S
	20 CLC
	30 ADC V
	40 SEC
	50 SBC #3
	60 STA S

Doubling a number:

BASIC example:	Machine code equivalent:
10 S = 2*S	10 ASL S

Expressions with parenthesis:

BASIC example:	Machine code equivalent:
10 S = 4*(K + 3)	10 LDA K
	20 CLC
	30 ADC #3
	40 ASL A
	50 ASL A
	60 STA S

Incrementing by 1:

BASIC example:	Machine code equivalent:
10 S = S + 1	10 INC S

Decrementing by 2:

BASIC example:	Machine code equivalent:
10 S = S − 2	10 DEC S
	20 DEC S

Calling a subroutine:

BASIC example:	Machine code equivalent:
10 GOSUB line	10 JSR label
100 RETURN	100 RTS

Clearing graphics:

BASIC example:	Machine code equivalent:
10 CLG	10 LDA #16
	20 JSR OSWRCH

Clearing text:

BASIC example:	Machine code equivalent:
10 CLS	10 LDA #12
	20 JSR OSWRCH

Printing text:

BASIC example:	Machine code equivalent:
10 MESSAGE =	10 LDX #0
"DANGER"	20 .BACK LDA MESSAGE,X
	30 JSR OSWRCH
	40 INX
	50 CPX #6
	60 BNE BACK

Note: The machine code shown depends on certain initial actions carried out in BASIC. Thus, we must use the string indirection operator to store the ASCII codes of the text: MESSAGE= "DANGER" and ensure that the text is located at the end of the program by setting MESSAGE=P%+n, where n is the number of bytes in the machine code program or a conservative estimate.

Wait for space key:

BASIC example:	Machine code equivalent:
10 K$ = GET$	10 .BACK JSR OSRDCH
20 IF K$ = " " THEN	20 CMP #32
GOTO 10	30 BNE BACK

Note: 32 is ASCII for space

Respond within 2 seconds:

BASIC example:	Machine code equivalent:
10 CITY$ = INKEY$(200)	10 LDX #200
	20 LDY #0
	30 LDA #&81
	40 JSR OSBYTE

Loop structure (advancing by 1):

BASIC example:	Machine code equivalent:
10 FOR S = 1 TO 50	10 LDX #1
.	20 .BACK ...
.	.
.	.
.	.
100 NEXT	.
	100 INX
	110 CPX #51
	120 BNE BACK

Loop structure (advancing by n):

BASIC example:	Machine code equivalent:
10 FOR S = 0 TO 20	
STEP 2	10 LDX #0
.	20 .BACK ...
.	.
.	.
100 NEXT	.
	100 INX
	110 INX
	120 CPX #22
	130 BNE BACK

Loop structure (reducing by 1):

BASIC example:	Machine code equivalent:
10 FOR S = 50 TO 1	
STEP −1	10 LDX #50
.	20 .BACK ...
.	.
.	.
100 NEXT	.
	100 DEX
	110 BNE BACK

Loop Structure (reducing by n):

    BASIC example: Machine code equivalent:

```
10 FOR S = 10 TO 1                 10 LDX #10
   STEP -2                         20 .BACK ...
   .                                  .
   .                                  .
   .                                  .
100 NEXT                              .
                                   100 DEX
                                   110 DEX
                                   120 BNE BACK
```

Loop structure with variable:

    BASIC example: Machine code equivalent:

```
10 FOR S = 1 TO BLOGS   10 LDX #1
   .                    20 .BACK ...
   .                       .
   .                       .
100 NEXT                   .
                        100 INX
                        110 CPX BLOGS+1
                        120 BNE BACK
```

Note: BLOGS must be a number greater than 1 but less than 128.

Loop structure with two variables:

    BASIC example: Machine code equivalent:

```
10 FOR S = N TO Z       10 LDX N
   .                    20 .BACK ...
   .                       .
   .                       .
100 NEXT                   .
                        100 INX
                        110 CPX Z+1
                        120 BNE BACK
```

Note: Z must be greater than N and both must be greater than 1 but less than 128.

Loop structure with decreasing variable:

BASIC example:	Machine code equivalent:
10 FOR S = N TO 1	
STEP −1	10 LDX N
.	20 .BACK …
.	.
.	.
100 NEXT	.
	100 DEX
	110 BNE BACK

Loop structure with two variables:

BASIC example:	Machine code equivalent:
10 FOR S = N TO Z	
STEP −1	10 LDX N
.	20 .BACK …
.	.
.	.
100 NEXT	.
	100 DEX
	110 CPX Z
	120 BNE BACK

Conditional to zero test:

BASIC example:	Machine code equivalent:
10 IF S = 0 THEN	
GOTO 200	10 LDA S
.	20 BEQ FORWARD
.	.
.	.
200 …	.
	100 .FORWARD …

Conditional to not-zero test:

BASIC example:	Machine code equivalent:
10 IF S <> 0 THEN	
GOTO 200	10 LDA S
.	20 BNE FORWARD
.	.
.	.
200	.
	100 .FORWARD …

Conditional to negative test:

BASIC example:

10 IF S < 0 THEN
 GOTO 200
 .
 .
 .
200

Machine code equivalent:

10 LDA S
20 BMI FORWARD
 .
 .
 .
100 .FORWARD

Conditional to greater than zero test:

BASIC example:

10 IF S > 0 THEN
 GOTO 200
 .
 .
 .
200

Machine code equivalent:

10 LDA S
20 BEQ ~~FORWARD~~ *BODY*
30 BPL FORWARD
40 . BODY
 .
 .
100 .FORWARD

Conditional to positive test:

BASIC example:

10 IF S >=0 THEN
 GOTO 200
 .
 .
 .
200

Machine code equivalent:

10 LDA S
20 BPL FORWARD
 .
 .
 .
100 .FORWARD

Change variable on positive test:

BASIC example:

IF S > = 0 THEN K = Z

Machine code equivalent:

10 LDA S
20 ~~BPL FORWARD~~ *BMI FORWARD*
30 LDA Z
40 STA K
 .
 .
 .
100 .FORWARD ...

Increment variable on negative test:

BASIC example:	Machine code equivalent:
10 IF S < 0 THEN K =	
K+1	10 LDA S
	20 ~~BMI FORWARD~~ *BPL FORNAR*
	30 INC K
	.
	.
	.
	100 .FORWARD ...

Change sign of variable on zero test:

BASIC example:	Machine code equivalent:
10 IF S = 0 THEN K = −K	10 LDA S
	20 BNE FORWARD
	30 LDA K
	40 EOR #&FF *% change bits*
	50 CLC
	60 ADC #1 *% add 1*
	70 STA K
	.
	.
	.
	100 .FORWARD ...

Note: Changing the sign means to replace with two's complement, so we reverse all the bits and add 1.

Conditional comparison test:

BASIC example:	Machine code equivalent:
10 IF K = Z THEN	
GOTO 500	10 LDA K
.	20 ~~CPM Z~~ *CMP Z*
.	30 BEQ FORWARD
.	.
500	.
	100 .FORWARD

Comparison to constant test:

BASIC example: Machine code equivalent:

10 IF S = 25 THEN K =
   K − G

```
10 LDA S
20 CMP #25
30 BNE FORWARD
40 LDA K
50 SEC
60 SBC G
70 STA K
  .
  .
  .
100 .FORWARD ...
```

Comparisons with AND connective:

BASIC example: Machine code equivalent:

10 IF S = 5 AND K = 23
   THEN GOTO 500
   .
   .
   .
500

```
10 LDA S
20 CMP #5
30 BNE NOTEQ
40 LDA K
50 CMP #23
60 BEQ FORWARD
70 .NOTEQ ...
  .
  .
  .
100 .FORWARD ...
```

Comparisons with OR connective:

BASIC example: Machine code equivalent:

10 IF S = 5 OR K = 23
   THEN GOTO 500
   .
   .
   .
500

```
10 LDA S
20 CMP #5
30 BEQ FORWARD
40 LDA K
50 CMP #23
60 BEQ FORWARD
  .
  .
  .
100 .FORWARD ...
```

Sound a short beep:

BASIC example:	Machine code equivalent:
10 VDU 7	10 LDA #7
	20 JSR OSWRCH

Move cursor down one line:

BASIC example:	Machine code equivalent:
10 VDU 10	10 LDA #10
	20 JSR OSWRCH

Move cursor up one line:

BASIC example:	Machine code equivalent:
10 VDU 11	10 LDA #11
	20 JSR OSWRCH

Forward cursor one space:

BASIC example:	Machine code equivalent:
10 VDU 9	10 LDA #9
	20 JSR OSWRCH

Backward cursor one space:

BASIC example:	Machine code equivalent:
10 VDU 8	10 LDA #8
	20 JSR OSWRCH

Turn on printer:

BASIC example:	Machine code equivalent:
10 VDU 2	10 LDA #2
	20 JSR OSWRCH

Turn off printer:

BASIC example:	Machine code equivalent:
10 VDU 3	10 LDA #3
	20 JSR OSWRCH

The software multiway switch:

BASIC example:	Machine code equivalent:
10 ON S GOTO 100,200,300	10 JSR OSRDCH
.	20 CMP #1
100 ...	30 BEQ DEST1
.	40 CMP #2
200 ...	50 BEQ DEST2
.	60 CMP #3
300 ...	70 BEQ DEST3

```
          .
          .
          .

100 .DEST1 ...

          .
          .

200 .DEST2 ...

          .
          .

300 .DEST3 ...
```

Indirection operators

Page 409 of the *User Guide* is concerned with rather frightening information on *indirection* operators. The word itself is distinctly unfriendly but its meaning is benign. The only trouble is the tendency to confuse it with *indirect* addressing which has an entirely different meaning.

An indirection operator is used when machine addresses are used to locate variables instead of leaving the operating system to arrange it automatically. For example, when we write in BASIC the line, A = 25, it is the operating system in the background which decides where to store the number 25 and how many bytes to use for it. In fact, although 25 is only a small number which is easily accommodated in a single storage byte, it will occupy five bytes because the variable 'A' is recognised by the interpreter as a floating point variable. Indirection operators allow us not only to choose the precise storage address but also the number of bytes used. Those of us who have used other machines, apart from the BBC model, will be familiar with the keywords PEEK and POKE which were, in fact, indirection operators although the term was not then used. The BBC machine version of BASIC does not include PEEK or POKE for indirection. Instead, the query (?), the pling(!) and the dollar sign($) are used. I think the term 'pling' may be unfamiliar to some readers (as it was to me before I read the *User Guide*) but apparently it is the posh word for the exclamation mark.

The operators have the following significance:

? is used for signifying *single* byte storage.
! is used for signifying four-byte storage (four bytes is one *word* in BBC BASIC).
$ is used for signifying character strings from 1 to 256 characters.

I found the use of these operators very confusing, having been weaned on PEEK and POKE, because it is only the *position* of these operators which distinguish whether you are peeking or poking.

The byte indirection operator

Some examples follow which show the position of the byte indirection operator. BLOGS = ?&0DFF will place the contents of address &0DFF into the variable BLOGS. This is the same as BLOGS = PEEK (&0DFF) in other BASICs. In contrast, ?&0DFF = BLOGS will place the contents of the variable BLOGS into the address &0DFF. This is the same as POKE &0DFF, BLOGS in other BASICs.

It is often required to input a variable from the keyboard and place it into one of the registers. There are several ways of doing this but they all involve byte indirection. It is often more convenient, and certainly easier, to use the normal INPUT statement in BASIC to input the variable because a prompt message is almost mandatory. After the variable has been entered, it can be transferred by an indirection operator into a machine address and subsequently loaded by machine code into the accumulator by LDA or in the X register by LDX. The following illustrates the procedure:

```
100 INPUT"ENTER MISSILE VELOCITY IN Km/sec"
    SPEED
110 ?&0DFF = SPEED :REM BYTE INDIRECTION
120 [
130 LDA &0DFF
```

It is, of course, the responsibility of the keyboard operator to ensure that the number entered for velocity is within the capacity of a single byte. A good programmer, of course, would include some kind of input validation loop to guard against improper magnitudes but to include such detail in our examples would appear so much trivia.

The word indirection operator

The BBC machine uses four bytes to hold BASIC integers. To relate this to machine code the word indirection operator is used in the following manner. BLOGS = !&0DF0 would place a four-byte length number into BLOGS from the consecutive memory addresses &0DF0,&0DF1,&0DF2 and &0DF3. The lowest significant byte is always the one stated in the operand (in this case &0DF0). The following example may help in the understanding.

Assume the contents of the four locations to be:

&0DF0 = 34
&0DF1 = 57
&0DF2 = B5
&0DF3 = 04

If we write PRINT BLOGS, we shall see a very large number, 878163204, and not the expected result. This is because the BASIC line PRINT BLOGS always converts everything to decimal. To confirm that nothing is amiss, use that funny little sign called the *tilde*. PRINT~BLOGS will cause the printout to be in hex. It will be &3457B504 if nothing has gone wrong.

The above description confirms that BLOGS = !&0DF0 is the four-byte equivalent of the byte indirection operator, equivalent to PEEK in other BASICs. The equivalent to POKE, using the same numerical addresses and variable names would be written: !&0DF0 = BLOGS. This would put the number defined by the variable BLOGS into the four consecutive addresses &0DF0, &0DF1,&0DF2 and &0DF3, the least significant digits in &0DF0.

The string indirection operator

It might be as well to remind you that the term 'string' in BASIC is used when referring to any character on the keyboard, such as the letters and punctuation marks as well as figures (although arithmetic processes cannot be carried out when figures are in string form). A collection of characters is also called a 'string' and the dollar sign is well known as the defining operator. Thus a string variable such as BLOOD$ can hold a string of characters such as the word "Haemoglobin". Note that the dollar sign is at the *end* of the variable – a very important point.

The string indirection operator also uses the dollar sign but at the *beginning* of the variable.

Example: $&0D00 = "Haemoglobin". Now what exactly will this do?

It will place each individual character (in ASCII form) into a consecutive block of addresses, the first letter 'H' going into the quoted address &0D00, the next letter 'a' into &0D01 and so on, until the final 'n' goes into &0D0A. This, the string indirection operator provides us with a very convenient tool for inserting messages or general text into machine locations. The following few lines show how text can be safely passed by BASIC into a machine address block:

```
100 INPUT"ENTER YOUR NAME "Name$
100 $&0D00 = Name$
```

Of course, if the person at the keyboard happens to have one of those long hyphenated names preceded by imposing titles there could be a byte shortage in memory. Remember that string indirection can handle up to 256 characters in one string. If text of this order is to be handled, it is well to use the space above BASIC for the machine code, using the DIM method. Here is an example:

```
100 DIM SPACE 500
110 $SPACE = "BLOOD"
```

The machine code area is given the starting address SPACE. We don't need to know the absolute hex address where the SPACE area starts because it is the responsibility of the operating system. Line 110 is the string indirection statement. Try typing PRINT $SPACE. You will get the word BLOOD on the screen. Now try typing PRINT ?SPACE and you will get the number 66 on the screen. This may appear mysterious until you realise that ?SPACE is the order to print the contents of the *starting* byte of the block SPACE. Since the text was BLOOD, it should print the ASCII for the first letter (B) which is 66. It is appreciated that much of this material is BASIC rather than machine-oriented but the BBC assembler is unique in having a close relationship with the interpreter. It would be pointless to use a lengthy block of STA immediate type instructions to store the ASCII code for each letter of text when it is so convenient to use the strong indirection operator. After all, the indirection operators are intended for machine code interaction so it is not really cheating to take advantage of them. Finally, it is worth drawing attention once more to the possible confusion which may arise regarding the position of the dollar sign. It is so easy to mix up normal string variable names with indirection operators, thus:

BLOGS$ is a normal string variable.
$BLOGS is using the string indirection form.

Speed considerations

Relative to BASIC, all machine code programs or segments of programs will be fast but some will be faster than others. When you are in the initial learning phase of machine code writing it is understandable that subtleties of coding will not play a large part in program construction. Getting a program to work at all is the overriding aim in the first few weeks or months. Nevertheless, it is worth delving into the principles governing program speed. It is mainly a question of keeping the coding within a loop as short as possible. Loops, by their very nature are the worst speed offenders because the same set of lines must be executed many times. Because of this, it obviously pays to make adequate preparations before entering a loop. Any operations which can be executed prior to loop entry will prevent those annoying delays. This advice is, of course, applicable to BASIC or any high-level language as well as machine code. There are, however, certain little rules which apply exclusively to machine code. Some of these are now discussed.

Effect of instruction cycles

Not all instructions take the same time to execute. The fundamental speed of any computer is determined by a quartz crystal which stabilises the frequency of the master timing pulses which are taken to various parts of the system. As mentioned in a previous chapter, the crystal frequency in the BBC machine is two million pulses per second (2 MHz in electronic engineering terms). The time for one clock pulse is therefore half a microsecond (0.5 μS) and this time is termed one clock *cycle*. It is convenient to express the speed of an individual instruction in terms of clock cycles – the more clock cycles required, the slower is the instruction execution time.

The manufacturers of the 6502 microprocessor publish, in the data sheets, the number of clock cycles required by each instruction. In fact, the data sheets are drenched with masses of data and one glance is enough to frighten the stoutest heart away from the subject. Too much detailed information in the early stages of any subject achieves the opposite of the effect intended. For this reason, a list of instruction clock cycles is not given in this book. Rough guidance can be more helpful than detail.

It would be very nice if we could say, for example, that LDA takes 2 clock cycles and that is the end of it. Unfortunately, this is not the case because the addressing mode used in the operand must be taken into consideration. In fact it is the addressing mode chosen which is the primary factor in determining the number of clock cycles. Wherever possible, use register to register transfers for temporary storage because no operand is required; the addressing is *implied*. This brings us to the first rule when choosing an addressing mode:

When choosing an addressing mode use implied addressing wherever possible.

Implied addressing, such as TAX,TXA,TYA etc. require only 2 clock cycles. For example, in the design of loops, try to use X or Y as the loop counter because DEX,DEY or INX or INY can be used to change the loop variable. Unfortunately, the accumulator cannot be incremented or decremented with an implied address mode; there is no INA or DEA. The only way would be to subtract 1 (or add 1) using immediate addressing which, although still only taking 2 clock cycles, will require one extra instruction to set or reset the carry as appropriate.

Apart from implied addressing, other instructions require an operand. The quickest addressing mode in the op-code-plus-operand type of instruction is *immediate*, which as we have just seen, takes only 2 clock cycles. There is, of course, a kind of penalty associated with this addressing mode – the operand must be a numerical constant. Even if it is an ASCII character code, it is still a constant so it must be restrictive in many applications. Whilst on the subject of constants, it is important to realise that all constants, even those written in decimal, are converted by the assembler into the corresponding hex code. Although we have frequently used decimal operands in our examples it is worth steeling yourself to use hex wherever possible when writing machine code. Although it is an unfamiliar notation, if you stick at it you will benefit in the long run. It is, after all, the 'natural' numbering system in machine code.

Direct, or absolute addressing takes at least 4 cycles, although one less if the reference is to page zero (0000 to 00FF hex). The shift and rotate instructions used are rather expensive if carried out on memory with direct or absolute addressing. They take 6 cycles in general but 5 if the reference is to page zero. We can, in fact, take this as a general rule – addresses in page zero will always take one clock cycle less than in any higher memory address. Unfortunately, not much of it is free (as we have discovered earlier).

Indexed addressing is powerful but because the index register has to go through an adding cycle it is understandable that 4 cycles are required in most instructions but in the case of the shift and rotate this is increased to 7 cycles.

There is a rather complicated addressing mode called *indexed indirect* and another called by a confusingly similar title, *indirect indexed*, but you may remember that we agreed to shelve these two until my second book – *Get More From BBC Micro Machine Code.*

Troubles with two-byte numbers

There is no denying that working out the correct contents of each byte, given a large decimal number, is a fiddling task. For example, it can be quite a problem in the early stages to handle high resolution graphics in machine code. The graphics screen on the BBC Micro is considered to be a matrix of pixels 0 to 1279 wide and 0 to 1023 high which means that, in general, we require to work in two-byte format. To understand how awkward this can be, try working out how the number 1000 decimal must be divided into low-byte, high-byte form. Here is the solution:

1000 decimal is held as 232 in low-byte and 3 in high-byte.

Does this make sense? It does if we realise that the high-byte is worth 256 times as much as the low-byte. To check this, examine the following working:

3 is in the high-byte so is worth $3 \times 256 = 768$
232 is in the low-byte $\qquad = 232$
Collectively, these are worth: $\qquad \underline{1000}$

This is the result, but it may not be immediately obvious how it was arrived at. Using pencil and paper arithmetic, we first divide the original number 1000 by 256. This gives us 3 with 232 over which means that the 3 goes in the high-byte and 232 in the low-byte. It may be helpful to spend an hour or so trying out simple exercises on byte allocation. There is no need to use pencil and paper when you have the BBC machine around because on pages 238 and 299 of the *User Guide* will be found two most useful aids in the form of DIV and MOD. They are well described so it is pointless to re-describe them here. Instead, examine Example 7.1 which is a simple program written in BASIC which provides good practice material. On entering a decimal number, it will print out the low-byte, high-byte forms in both decimal and hex.

```
10 REM EXAMPLE 7.1
20 REM Low-byte,high-byte conversion
30 CLS
40 REPEAT
50 INPUT"Enter a number "N
60 PRINT"Low byte =  " N MOD 256
70 PRINT"High byte = " N DIV 256
80 PRINT
90 PRINT"In hex,these become:"
100 PRINT"Low byte =  "~N MOD 256
110 PRINT"High byte = "~N DIV 256
120 PRINT
130 UNTIL 2=3
```

Example 7.1. Converting numbers to two-byte form.

The largest number it can handle is limited by two-byte capacity which is 65,535 in decimal. On entering this number, the program will print out:

Low byte = 255
High byte = 255

In hex, these become:

Low byte = FF
High byte = FF

Since the number is FFFF in hex, the binary equivalent is 1111 1111 1111 1111.

&FF   1111 1111

232
128
1 04
  64
  40

0 0 0 0 1 0 0 0
0 1 1 1 0 1 0 1
1 0 0 1 1 0 0 0
1 0 1 1 1 1 0 0

00 1 1
00 1 0
01 1 0
0 L 0 0

256
1024

4096
8192
32

The program is intended for practice but there is an even shorter cut which exploits the truly remarkable assembler in the machine. It is possible to use any of the BASIC keywords to modify operands even within the assembly brackets. We have avoided using this facility in most of the previous examples because the primary

```
10 REM EXAMPLE 7.2 DRAW LINE
20 MODE 4
30 P%=&0D00
40 OSWRCH=&FFEE
50 [
60 LDA #25
70 JSR OSWRCH
80
90 LDA #4
100 JSR OSWRCH
110 LDA # 200 MOD 256
120 JSR OSWRCH
130 LDA # 200 DIV 256
140 JSR OSWRCH
150 LDA # 200 MOD 256
160 JSR OSWRCH
170 LDA # 200 DIV 256
180 JSR OSWRCH
190
200 LDA #25
210 JSR OSWRCH
220
230 LDA #5
240 JSR OSWRCH
250 LDA # 1000 MOD 256
260 JSR OSWRCH
270 LDA # 1000 DIV 256
280 JSR OSWRCH
290 LDA # 200 MOD 256
300 JSR OSWRCH
310 LDA # 200 DIV 256
320 JSR OSWRCH
330
340 RTS
350 ]
360 CLS
370 CALL &0D00
380END
```

Example 7.2. Draw line using MOD and DIV.

intention has been to *learn* machine code techniques. Since this book is nearing completion there is little point in pursuing restrictive practices any further. For example, we can include the MOD and DIV keywords within machine code programs to relieve us of the tedium of working out the above byte allocation.

Suppose, within a program, we want to draw a line in MODE 4

```
 10 REM EXAMPLE 7.3 RANDOM TRIANGLES
 20 MODE 2
 30 REPEAT
 40 GCOL 0,RND(16)
 50 P%=&0D00
 60 OSWRCH=&FFEE
 70 [
 80 OPT 0
 90 LDA #25
100 JSR OSWRCH
110 LDA #4
120 JSR OSWRCH
130 LDA # RND(1000)MOD 256
140 JSR OSWRCH
150 LDA # RND(1000)DIV 256
160 JSR OSWRCH
170 LDA # RND(1000)MOD 256
180 JSR OSWRCH
190 LDA # RND(1000)DIV 256
200 JSR OSWRCH
210 LDA #25
220 JSR OSWRCH
230 LDA #85
240 JSR OSWRCH
250 LDA # RND(1000)MOD 256
260 JSR OSWRCH
270 LDA # RND(1000)DIV 256
280 JSR OSWRCH
290 LDA # RND(1000)MOD 256
300 JSR OSWRCH
310 LDA # RND(1000)DIV 256
320 JSR OSWRCH
330 RTS
340 ]
350 CALL &0D00
360 CLG
370 UNTIL 2=3
```

Example 7.3. Random triangles.

graphics using the machine code equivalent of PLOT 5,X,Y. From page 378 of the *User Guide* we know that this will draw a line from the last referenced co-ordinates to X,Y. The assembly lines would take the form:

```
LDA #5
JSR OSWRCH
LDA #X MOD 256
JSR OSWRCH
LDA #X DIV 256
JSR OSWRCH
LDA #Y MOD 256
JSR OSWRCH
LDA #Y DIV 256
JSR OSWRCH
```

The complete listing is shown in Example 7.2.

Finally study Example 7.3 which illustrates well how BASIC keywords can be combined in assembly lines. It draws random coloured triangles over the screen.

Appendix A
List of 6502 Assembly Mnemonics

To avoid complication, no distinction is made between 'page zero' and absolute addressing.

Mnemonic Code	Action	Adressing details
TAX	Copy contents of A to X	
TXA	Copy contents of X to A	
TAY	Copy contents of A to Y	
TYA	Copy contents of Y to A	
INX	Add 1 to X	
INY	Add 1 to Y	
DEX	Subtract 1 from X	
DEY	Subtract 1 from Y	
TSX	Copy contents of SP to X	
TXS	Copy contents of X to SP	
PHA	Push A onto stack	
PLA	Pull A from stack	All op-codes in this section use *implicit* addressing. They have no operands.
PHP	Push PSR onto stack	
PLP	Pull PSR from stack	
CLC	Clear C bit in PSR	
SEC	Set C bit in PSR	
CLV	Clear V bit in PSR	
SED	Set D bit in PSR	
CLD	Clear D bit in PSR	
SEI	Set I bit in PSR	
CLI	Clear I bit in PSR	
NOP	No operation at all	
RTS	Return from subroutine	
RTI	Return from interrupt	
BRK	Break (stop)	

Mnemonic Code	Action	Addressing details
BNE	Branch if not equal	All op-codes in this section use *relative* addressing.
BEQ	Branch if equal	
BPL	Branch is positive (plus)	
BMI	Branch if negative (minus)	The operand can be an arbitrary chosen label.
BCC	Branch if C=0	
BCS	Branch if C=1	
BVC	Branch if V=0	Branching depends on the result of the *previous* instruction.
BVS	Branch if V=1	
LDA	Load A	All op-codes in this section use either immediate, absolute or indexed addressing.
ADC	Add with carry	
SBC	Subtract with carry	
CMP	Compare contents of A with	
AND	Perform logical AND	Either the X or Y register can be used for indexing. All results are in A.
ORA	Perform logical OR	
EOR	Perform logical Exclusive-OR.	
STA	Store A contents of with spec. address	As above but without immediate addressing.
STX	Store X	Absolute or indexed by Y addressing
STY	Store Y	Absolute or indexed by X addressing
LDX	Load X	Immediate, absolute or indexed by Y addressing.
LDY	Load Y	Immediate, absolute or indexed by X addressing.
CPX	Compare X contents of with number or contents of address	Immediate and absolute addressing.
CPY	Compare Y	Immediate and absolute addressing.

Mnemonic Code	Action	Addressing details
ASL	Arithmetic shift left	These can act on A alone
LSR	Logical shift right	or on memory using
ROL	Rotate left	absolute or indexed by
ROR	Rotate right	X addressing.
INC	Add 1 to memory	Absolute or indexed by
DEC	Subtract 1 from memory	X addressing.
BIT	Bit test on memory	Absolute addressing.
JMP	Jump to absolute address	Absolute addressing.
JSR	Jump to subroutine	

Appendix B
ASCII Character Codes (Modes 0-6)

Decimal	Hex	Character	Decimal	Hex	Character	Decimal	Hex	Character
32	20	Space	64	40	@	96	60	£
33	21	!	65	41	A	97	61	a
34	22	"	66	42	B	98	62	b
35	23	#	67	43	C	99	63	c
36	24	$	68	44	D	100	64	d
37	25	%	69	45	E	101	65	e
38	26	&	70	46	F	102	66	f
39	27	'	71	47	G	103	67	g
40	28	(	72	48	H	104	68	h
41	29	)	73	49	I	105	69	i
42	2A	*	74	4A	J	106	6A	j
43	2B	+	75	4B	K	107	6B	k
44	2C	,	76	4C	L	108	6C	l
45	2D	−	77	4D	M	109	6D	m
46	2E	.	78	4E	N	110	6E	n
47	2F	/	79	4F	O	111	6F	o
48	30	0	80	50	P	112	70	p
49	31	1	81	51	Q	113	71	q
50	32	2	82	52	R	114	72	r
51	33	3	83	53	S	115	73	s
52	34	4	84	54	T	116	74	t
53	35	5	85	55	U	117	75	u
54	36	6	86	56	V	118	76	v
55	37	7	87	57	W	119	77	w
56	38	8	88	58	X	120	78	x
57	39	9	89	59	Y	121	79	y
58	3A	:	90	5A	Z	122	7A	z
59	3B	;	91	5B	]	123	7B	{
60	3C	<	92	5C	\	124	7C		
61	3D	=	93	5D	]	125	7D	}
62	3E	>	94	5E	∧	126	7E	~
63	3F	?	95	5F	_	127	7F	Delete

Appendix C
Where to Locate Machine Code

FIXED ABSOLUTE ADDRESS BANDS BELOW &E00	
Hex addresses	Sacrifices
&900–&AFF (512 locations)	Cannot use cassette tape on OPENIN/OPENOUT commands. Cannot use RS423 serial interface. Normal SAVE and LOAD commands are still usable.
&C00–CFF (256 locations)	Cannot use *programmed* characters under the extended ASCII codes 223–255 inclusive.
&B00–&BFF (256 locations)	Cannot use the programmable keys.
&D00 to &DFF (256 locations)	Quite safe providing disk interface is not used.
&70–&8F (32 locations)	These are page zero locatiaons free from the demands of the operating system.

DYNAMIC ALLOCATION OF ADDRESS SPACE
Below BASIC: First type PAGE = PAGE + 256 Then P% = PAGE − 256   (256 locations)
Above BASIC: First type LOMEM = LOMEM + 250 Then P% = TOP   (256 locations)
Type P% = TOP + 1000 (The extra 1000 allows for BASIC dynamic variables which should be sufficient for most programs)
Type DIM P% N% where N% is the number of bytes to be reserved.

Appendix D
Binary and Hex Summary

Capacity of single byte

- The largest unsigned integer in one byte = FF hex or 255 decimal.
- The largest positive two's complement number = 7F hex or +127 decimal.
- The largest negative two's complement number = 80 hex or −128 decimal.
- The largest number in BCD format = 99 hex or 99 decimal.

Absolute addresses

- The total address range = 0000 hex to FFFF hex = 0 to 65,535 decimal.
- One *page* of memory = 256 bytes. Four pages = 1K of memory.
- In the general address &PPZZ, PP is the page and ZZ the address on the page.
- There are 256 pages in a 64K address map.
- The 6502 stack is situated in page 1, &0100 to &01FF.
- Paged ROMs, including the BASIC interpreter, are situated in pages &80 to &B0.
- Operating system ROM is situated in pages &C0 to &FB.
- Memory mapped input/output is situated in page &FC.
- The remainder of the operating system ROM is situated in page &FF.

Appendix E
Operating System Subroutines

Name	Address	Objective	Parameter passing
OSRDCH	&FFE0	To read character from selected input stream.	Inputs into A.
OSWRCH	&FFEE	Writes character and/or control codes to selected output stream. All VDU commands can be driven. (See page 378 in the *User Guide*)	Outputs from A. If more than one control code is required they must be passed via A one at a time to OSWRCH.
OSBYTE	&FFF4	Produces a variety of machine operating system actions. The *FX commands can be driven. (See page 418 in the *User Guide*.)	First parameter must be in A, second in X and third in Y before calling OSBYTE. X and Y are set to zero if only one parameter is required.
OSWORD	&FFF1	Produces more complex operating system actions, requiring many parameters, such as sound effects, timers, elapsed time clock, pixel colours and dot patterns. (See page 458 in the *User Guide*.)	Control code in A. Address of parameter block in X and Y, low-byte in X.

Glossary of Terms

Absolute address: the numerical number identifying an address.

Accumulator: the main register within the microprocessor and the only one equipped for arithmetic.

Address bus: the 16 lines from the microprocessor which activate the selected memory location or device.

Address: a number which is associated with a particular memory location. This number can be in decimal or hexadecimal.

ANDgate: a gate which delivers a logic 1 out only if all inputs are logic 1.

Anding: using a mask to ensure selected bits become or remain 0.

Assembler mnemonics: a three-letter group uniquely defining an op-code.

Assembler: a program which converts a program written in assembly code to the equivalent machine code.

Base address: the operand address of an indexed instruction.

Base: the number of different characters used in a counting system. Decimal is base 10, binary is base 2 and hex is base 16.

Bit: one of the two possible states of a binary counting system, 1 or 0.

Block diagram: a simplified diagram of an electrical system using interconnected labelled boxes.

Boolean algebra: a strange kind of algebra used by electronic engineers to handle switching systems (see logic gates).

Byte: a group of 8 bits.

Chip: accepted slang for an integrated circuit.

Compiler: system software which translates a program written in high-level language into a machine code equivalent. The entire program is translated before it is run.

Data bus: the 8 lines from the microprocessor which carry the data to and from memory or external devices.

Decimal: the normal counting system using the ten characters 0,1,...9.

Direct addressing: the operand is a two-byte address as distinct from zero page addressing which is a single byte address. Also called *absolute addressing.*

Disassembler: a program which will display a machine code program in assembly language. The opposite process to assembly.

Effective address: the sum of the base and relative address.

Exclusive OR gate: a gate which delivers a logic 1 only if the inputs are at different logic states.

Exclusive or-ing: using a mask to ensure selected bits assume the opposite state.

Firmware: programs already in ROM.

Flag: a single bit used to indicate whether something has happened or not (see program status register).

Handshaking: a term used to describe the method of synchronising an external device to the computer.

Hardware: all the bits and pieces of a computer such as the chips, circuit board, keys, etc. That which you can see, feel and break!

Hex: see hexadecimal.

Hexadecimal: a counting system using sixteen characters 0,1...9,A, B,C,D,E,F.

High byte: the most significant half of a two-byte number.

High-level language: a language written in the form of statements, each statement being equivalent to many machine code instructions. BASIC is a high-level language.

Immediate addressing: the operand is the data itself rather than an address.

Implicit address: see implied address.

Implied address: an address which is inherent in the op-code, therefore requiring no following operand.

Index register: either the X or Y register when used to modify an address.

Indexed address: an address which has been formed by the addition of an index register's contents.

Integer: a whole number without a fraction.

Integrated circuit: a chip containing a number of interconnected circuits.

Interpreter: system software which translates and executes each high-level language statement separately. BASIC is normally interpreted although compiler versions exist.

Logic gates: electrical circuits which behave as switches. The input conditions determine whether the switch is 'open' or 'closed'.

Low-byte: the least significant half of a two-byte number.

Low-level language: a series of codes rather than a language, each line resulting in one order to the microprocessor.

lsb: the least significant bit in the byte (the rightmost bit).

LSI: large scale integration. Normally taken to mean in the order of tens of thousands of circuits on a single chip. The 6502 microprocessor is LSI.

SSI: small scale integration. Normally taken to mean a few circuits, often simple logic gates, on a single chip.

Machine code: strictly, this term should be used for instructions written in binary but is now used loosely to include hex coding and assembly language.

Mask: a bit pattern used in conjunction with either AND, EOR or ORA to act on selected bits within a byte.

Microprocessor: the integrated circuit which is the central processor or 'brain' of the computer. The BBC machine uses the 6502 species.

Mnemonic: code groups chosen so we can memorise them easily.

msb: the most significant bit in the byte (the leftmost bit).

MSI: medium scale integration. Normally taken to mean up to a few hundred circuits on a single chip.

Nibble: a group of 4 bits.

Nybble: see nibble.

Object code: the translated version of the source code.

One's complement: a number formed by changing the state of all bits in a register.

Op-code: abbreviation for operational code. It is that part of a machine code instruction which tells the computer what kind of action is required.

Operand: that part of a machine code instruction which gives the data or where to find the data.

Operating system: the software already in ROM which is designed to help you use the computer.

OR gate: a gate which delivers a logic 1 out if any one or more inputs are logic 1.

Oring: using a mask to ensure selected bits become or remain 1.

Page one address: any address within the range 256 to 511 decimal or 0100 to 01FF hex.

PC: see program counter.

Program counter: the only 16-bit register in the 6502. Contains the address of the next instruction byte.

Program status register: a register containing flag bits which indicate if overflow, carries etc. have been caused by the previous instruction.

PSR: see program status register.

Relative address: the contents of the index register.

Resident assembler: an assembler which is already in ROM when you purchase the machine.

Resident subroutines: those in ROM which you can use, providing you know their starting address.

ROM: abbreviation for Read Only Memory. Information stored is permanent even when the power supply is off.

Rotate: similar to shift but any bit pushed out from the carry is reinserted at the other end.

Shift: to move the bit pattern, one place to the left or right.

Signed binary: the binary system which uses the msb as a sign bit.

Silicon chip: most chips are fabricated from a silicon base although some of the super-fast modern varieties may be using a mixture of gallium and arsenic.

Software: general term for all programs.

Source code: the program in its high-level form.

Subroutine: a program segment which will normally have general purpose use and which can be used in other programs.

Symbolic address: an arbitrary chosen name used in place of the numerical address. It is only recognised if it has been previously assigned to this number.

Two pass assembly: passing the source code twice through the assembler. Essential if branches are to forward addresses.

Two's complement: a number formed by adding 1 to the one's complement. Used for negative number representation.

Unsigned integer: a binary number without using the msb as a sign bit.

User port: one of the output sockets which can be used to control your own special devices.

User subroutines: subroutines which you make up for yourself.

Volatile memory: one which loses all data when power is interrupted.

X-register: a general-purpose register which can be used in indexed addressing.

Y-register: similar to X-register.

Zero page address: any address within the range 0 to 255 decimal or 00 to FF hex.

Index